Tomorrow's Church Today

Title: Tomorrow's church today : the way forward / edited by
 Michael Kelly.

ISBN: 9781925486377 (paperback)
       9781925486384 (hardback)
       9781925486391 (ebook : epub)
       9781925486407 (ebook : Kindle)
       9781925486414 (ebook : pdf)

Notes: Includes bibliographical references.

Subjects: Catholic Church.
 Church management.

Other Creators/Contributors:
 Kelly, Michael 1953 January 16- editor.

Dewey Number: 282

Cover design and Layout by Astrid Sengkey

Text Minion Pro Size 10 &11

Published by:

An imprint of the ATF Press Publishing
Group owned by ATF (Australia) Ltd.
PO Box 504
Hindmarsh, SA 5007
ABN 90 116 359 963
www.atfpress.com
Making a lasting difference

Tomorrow's Church Today
The Way Forward

Edited by Michael Kelly SJ

ATF Theology
Adelaide
2016

Table of Contents

Introduction

Change is never organised. It always comes unexpectedly. Whether it's personal, political, cultural or economic, it is always triggered by the aberrant, unplanned and unpredictable event or person.

Such has been the case with the Catholic Church. And nowhere is it more obvious than with what Jorge Mario Bergoglio has unbuttoned in the Catholic Church. The unknown figure from Argentina was thought by many of his Jesuit confreres to be an authoritarian cult figure. In ecclesiastical terms, he seemed to fit with the Vatican narrative about liberation theology—it was a bad thing.

And despite all that, he has unleashed a torrent of change in the Catholic Church about which there is only one question: can it last and is it sustainable? Admirable and even desired as it may be, can it last? Is this Pontificate a flash in the pan with no sustainable achievements or underpinning? Style rather than substance?

This volume of essays says why it will, how it can and why it must.

Massimo Faggioli explains what essential questions about the Church—that have their authoritative answers in Vatican II—are addressed and responded to in the priorities of this Pontificate.

Geraldine Doogue looks at the issues that vex today's Catholics and cry out for a positive response. Robert Mickens sees the life of the Vatican from the inside and examines what can happen to effect the change.

Geoffrey Robinson looks to the New Testament and beyond for ways to address what will take the Church forward in contemporary society on an issue that disturbs so many—divorce and remarriage in the Church. Antony Campbell targets some central statuses and offices in the Church that need basic overhaul if the Church is to move forward.

Bishop William Morris, a victim of the Vatican's unaccountable system of administration, looks at why we can and should put the rubbish behind us.

This is a hopeful book that suggests a chart we can follow for the renewal and reform of Catholicism in the twenty-first century.

Michael Kelly, SJ

Mission and Governance of a Global Catholic Church: Revival and Completion of Vatican II

Massimo Faggioli

Introduction: Church Governance and Francis' Synodal Process 2014–2015

The Catholic Church needs to be governed. We are past the delusions of a purely communitarian, self-governing Catholicism where the pure spiritual quality of the Church members is a safeguard strong enough against the corruption of the institutional level. The beginning of the twenty-first century has been a particularly important learning moment for the Church: the sex abuse crisis has shown the corruption of the system but also the urgent need for an effective Church government. The election of Pope Francis in March 2013 is also part of a change in the perception of the importance of Church government, after the twenty-seven year of charismatic pontificate of John Paul II.[1]

From the point of view of the relationship between ecclesiology and governance of the Church, the pontificate of pope Francis is a complex mix. The conciliar Catholicism of Jorge Mario Bergoglio is partly a recovery of Vatican II and partly the reckoning with the shortcomings of Vatican II. Francis' view of the Church is one that has received the ecclesiological shift of Vatican II and makes a creative synthesis between what Vatican II settled, what the Council talked about but did not settle, and what Vatican II did not even talk about.[2] Francis has recovered in particular one of the intuitions of Vatican

---

1. See Andrea Riccardi, *Governo carismatico. 25 anni di pontificato* (Milano: Mondadori, 2003).
2. About this see Massimo Faggioli, *Pope Francis: Tradition in Transition* (New York: Paulist, 2015).

II in terms of theological method: the idea of communal process over bureaucratic decision, of spiritual discernment over magisterial authoritarianism, and of open-ended thinking over the obsession about continuity as opposed to discontinuity.[3]

This shift embodied by Francis has become visible especially with the two-year synodal process celebrated in October 2014 and October 2015 with the gathering of bishops in Rome and with a long synodal intersession between the end of the first synod and the beginning of the second. Both the synods of 2014–2015 and synodal intersessions have been an absolute first since the creation of the Bishops' Synod by Paul VI on September 15 1965, at the beginning of the fourth and last session of Vatican II. Pope Francis' synodal process has shown a few features of the present state of the Catholic Church—the difficulty to lift the veil on the shallow consensus the bishops were supposed to have and to finally address the call to reality that challenges many assumptions about the life of Catholics.

But the synodal process has also highlighted the emergencies for the governance of the global Catholic Church. This is something that pope Francis himself acknowledged with the speech of October 17 2015—the most important speech of a pope on synodality to date.[4] The acknowledgment of the theological and institutional emergencies and the need for a new phase in the governance of the global Catholic Church requires also a new phase in the reflection of theologians in this moment of new open spaces in the life of the Church.

This is the reason for a new appraisal of the relationship between the potential of Vatican II and the needs of the governance of today's Church. At the same time, we need to keep in mind the necessity for the Church to be an agent of evangelization and not of preservation of the institutional self. This essay tries to capture four essential tensions for a new ecclesiological appraisal of the issue of Church governance: collegiality and synodality; institution and community; ministry and people of God; center and periphery.

---

3. See Antonio Spadaro SJ, 'Intervista a Papa Francesco', *La Civiltà Cattolica* 3918 (19 September 2013), 449–77. English version: 'A Big Heart Open to God', in *America*, 19 September 2013.

4. Francis, Address at the ceremony commemorating the fiftieth anniversary of the institution of the Synod of Bishops, October 17, 2015 http://w2.vatican. va/content/francesco/en/speeches/2015/october/documents/papa-francesco_20151017_50-anniversario-sinodo.html.

Collegiality and Synodality

Collegiality is one of the most important fruits of the Second Vatican Council, but to a large extent it has remained a symbolic fruit. The way it was phrased at Vatican II (in the third chapter of the constitution *Lumen Gentium*) and the way it was received and institutionally implemented after Vatican II require now substantial updates in light of a key theological dimension of the Church, 'synodality', that was not debated at Vatican II.

It is true that Vatican II was instrumental in the decision of Paul VI to create the Bishops' Synod in 1965. But the Byshops' Synod was created as an instrument of papal primacy and of episcopal collegiality, and not an instrument of the Church's fundamental 'synodality'—the particular communional way of the Church to prepare, formulate, receive, and understand decisions in and for the Church. It is not surprising that at Vatican II there was no talk of synodality in the sense the word means today. The ecclesiological shift of Vatican II was dominated by episcopal collegiality, which remains limited at the level of the episcopate. But with his speech of 17 October 2015, but also with his leadership of the Bishops' Synods of 2014 and 2015, Francis showed us a remarkable example of a reception of Vatican II that expands on the basis of the *intentio legentis*. He brings the eyes of those who read Vatican II in their actual existential and cultural situation and of the needs of the Church.

The first dimension to be considered is therefore the relationship between collegiality and synodality. 'Episcopal collegiality' at Vatican II means that the papacy and the college of bishops work collegially in order to develop reflections necessary for the government of the Church. On the one hand, at Vatican II collegiality is technically a *modus operandi* that the pope chooses, not the bishops.[5] On the other

---

5. 'But the college or body of bishops has no authority unless it is understood together with the Roman Pontiff, the successor of Peter as its head. The pope's power of primacy over all, both pastors and faithful, remains whole and intact. In virtue of his office, that is as Vicar of Christ and pastor of the whole Church, the Roman Pontiff has full, supreme and universal power over the Church. And he is always free to exercise this power. The order of bishops, which succeeds to the college of apostles and gives this apostolic body continued existence, is also the subject of supreme and full power over the universal Church, provided we understand this body together with its head the Roman Pontiff and never without this head. This power can be exercised only with the consent of the Roman

hand, collegiality is typical of a 'guild', of a separate group—only the bishops.

Vatican II did not articulate properly the relationship between *collegio episcoporum* and *communio ecclesiarum*,[6] and already at the end of the twentieth century it became clear that collegiality must be integrated with synodality.[7] The incompleteness of Vatican II about collegiality and synodality was made worse by the practices of the post-conciliar popes. The college of bishops has been largely seen as the rubber stamp of papal primacy. Episcopal collegiality has meant (until Francis) something 'affective' without being 'effective'.[8] There is here a direct link between collegiality and governance that affects the position and power of the central government of the Church in the Vatican.

The Roman Curia was created to strengthen the power of the pope, and in recent times the Curia in its actual state has in fact damaged the authority of the pope in the global Church. The Roman Curia has proven to be a liability for the authority of papal primacy because of the link between the primacy and the identification of the Curia as part of the primacy. In a culture of government that left collegiality only the demonstration of the bishops' affection for the pope, there was no room for synodal expressions of the whole Church's participation to the decision-making process.

Pontiff': Vatican II, constitution *Lumen Gentium*, par. 22 (21 November 1964) (http://www.vatican.va/archive/hist_councils/ii_vatican_council/documents/vat-ii_const_19641121_lumen-gentium_en.html.

6. See Hervé Legrand, 'Les évêques, les Églises locales et l'Église entière. Evolutions institutionnelles depuis Vatican II et chantiers actuels de recherche', in *Revue de Sciences Philosophiques et Théologiques*, 85 (2001): 461–509.

7. About this, see *Synod and Synodality: Theology, History, Canon Law and Ecumenism in New Contact. International Colloquium Bruges 2003*, edited by Alberto Melloni and Silvia Scatena (Münster: LIT, 2005).

8. About this distinction, see Joseph A Komonchak, 'The Roman Working Paper on Episcopal Conferences', in *Episcopal Conferences: Historical, Canonical and Theological Studies*, edited by Thomas J Reese (Washington, DC: Georgetown University Press, 1989), 177–204. On 1 April 2014, in a message to Cardinal Lorenzo Baldisseri, secretary general of the Synod of Bishops, Pope Francis spoke of the synod as an institution in terms of 'affective and effective collegiality', adding a significant 'effective' to the more typical (in the post-Vatican II period) 'affective'. See *Bollettino: Sala stampa della Santa Sede*, 8 April 2014, http://press. vatican.va/content/salastampa/en/bollettino/pubblico/2014/04/08/0251/00559. html.

There is little doubt that one of the long-term ecclesiological trajectories for the Catholic Church is towards a *synodal Church*: in the Church there are some issues that deserve to be matter of a larger process of reflection and discernment, not just limited to the pope and the bishops, but involving the clergy and the laity (meaning also women). The non-episcopal component of the Catholic Church (priests, monks and brothers/sisters in religious orders, laity) have received fewer and fewer opportunities to express themselves on some pressing issues that are thought out and decided in the Vatican. The Roman Catholic Church today is expected to be less clerical with more lay faithful and women in leadership positions. However, the disconnect between some magisterial pronouncements and large portions of the world Church is also a fruit of a lack of synodality in the Church.

Institution and Communion

The shift in ecclesiology from an institutionalist and juridical view of the Church to a more biblical, spiritual, and 'communional' understanding of the Church is undeniable. But we cannot forget that the Second Vatican Council took place in a moment in time when the Church as an institution felt still very sure of itself. The debates and the final documents approved at Vatican II framed the life of the Church largely in institutional terms, that is, a Church whose leadership was *clerical*, whose articulation was more *territorial* than personal, and whose *public standing* was as both partner and counterpart of the nation state which between the nineteenth and the twentieth centuries had replaced the empires. It is therefore an institution that was changing at Vatican II. But in reality, the role of the institution was not entirely different from the role it had for the members of the Church over previous centuries.

Fifty years after Vatican II it is clear that the Church in the world of today lives in profoundly changed conditions. To name a few, secularization and the neutrality of the state towards religion, the end of the 'Constantinian age', and the growing religious pluralism in most states around the globe are all part of these changed circummstances. And these changes challenge the institutional framework described by the bishops for the Church in the first half of the 1960s.

This institutional configuration of the Catholic Church has been changing during the post-Vatican II period even if the institution has resisted adapting to the new conditions and pretended that Church structures that were created for European Christendom can still serve the global Catholic Church today.

One of the typical products of the pre-Vatican II era was the concordates, bilateral juridical agreements between the Holy See and a nation state that guarantees the Catholic Church some privileges (that other churches and religions do not enjoy) and guarantees the state the loyal cooperation of the Church. The future of this juridical tool, typical of the Catholic tradition, was not part of the debate at Vatican II; concordates between the Holy See and important states (Italy in 1929 and Germany in 1933, just to name two) are not going to be abrogated soon. But this does not mean that the Catholic Church can ignore the deeply changed conditions of co-existence between Church and state.

It is clear that global Catholicism is going to remain a greatly diverse community of communions, all living in different juridical and political situations around the world. What is important to emphasize here is that the changes affecting the Church have affected its partner, the nation state, in an even more profound way. The 1960s were, with decolonization, the age of the final collapse of the colonial empires and the rise of new states. Fifty years later, the idea of the nation state is in a deep crisis and the Church needs to understand that its role changes now that the other member of the couple, that is, the nation state, is in this serious crisis.

Historically, Church and state/empire have coexisted for centuries and we need to think about what kind of Catholic Church there can be in states that are failed, semi-failed, members of strong international communities or isolated from the international community, and so on with the all possible variations that political scientists can provide us with. This is to say that we need to rediscover the complex mix of institutional and communional aspects of the Catholic Church. The institutional side of the Church is the one that is supposed to be vigilant on the abuses. A purely communional Church is something that is not adequate to the concrete, historical experience of the members of the Roman Catholic Church.

This is not a call to keep the status quo or to over-institutionalize the life of the Church. There are recent experiences within Catholicism that are perfect examples of the need for the Church to let the Spirit work. The phenomenon of the 'new ecclesial movements' corresponds to the need for the Church to see itself not only organised with a territorial system but also with a personal criterion, in communities not necessarily defined by a terriroty but that are made of people. The new movements also bring in a new kind of leadership in the Church that is not clerical. The Roman Catholic Church today is less based on the structures of Church government (dioceses), less institutional and territorial, and it relies more on movements, groups, and associations. These have a varied relationship with the institution and its local and central government, something is also down to an increased mobility of the faithful.

The sympathy of the post-Vatican II papacy towards the new forms of Christian life in 'movements' and associations has been translated only in a limited way in the central government of the Church, limiting also the transparency and accountability of some of these new ecclesial bodies (for example, Legionaries of Christ). But the relationship between the Church as an institution and these new movements is complex: they need each other and the charisms of these new movements flourished originally within the institutional Church.[9]

Leadership/Ministry and People of God

The modern emphasis on leadership has become pervasive in our political discourse, but also in the vocabulary of our education system. In this sense, there is a tension between the old idea of membership and citizenship on one side and the urge (that sometimes becomes an obsession in the age of neo-authoritarianism and crisis of democracy) on the other side to identify and rely on leadership. The ideas of leadership and membership/citizenship both apply to the Catholic Church: *citizenship* in the sense of responsible, individual and collective subjectivity in the communion of the faithful, and

---

9. See Massimo Faggioli, *Sorting Out Catholicism: Brief History of the New Ecclesial Movements* (Collegeville: Liturgical Press, 2014) and *The Rising Laity: Ecclesial Movements since Vatican II* (Mahwah NJ-New York: Paulist Press, 2016).

leadership in the sense of visible and accountable roles of guidance in the Church that discern the signs of the times and are attentive to the Holy Spirit and to the leadership of the whole people of God.

This relationship between leadership and citizenship is at the same time old and new in Church history. What is certainly new is the emphasis in our culture about leadership. The first few years of the post-Vatican II period were marked by a stress on the popular, collective leadership in the Church of the whole people of God, also in reaction to centuries of clericalism. In the second phase of the post-Vatican II period, one of the counter-balancing contributions of John Paul II was certainly the assertion of an old-style clerical leadership of the Church that was not contradicted by the approval of a new style of a leader or principal person in a movement, cause, etc in lay movements in the Church.

The pontificate of Francis is casting a new light on the relationship between leadership and people in the Church. It is clear on the one hand that the Church needs leadership. On the other hand, the ecclesiological debate since Vatican II and the tragedy of the sex abuse crisis has shown the kind of leadership the Church needs. Francis has renewed the Church's confidence in the idea of leadership because he embodies a sense of leadership that is not loyal to the institutional status quo but is a prophetic leader. He has spoken repeatedly about the kind of leader the Church needs, focusing especially on clerical leadership speaking in unforgiving terms about the counter-witness given by many in the hierarchy.[10]

The issue becomes more complicated when we have to figure out the other part of the picture. The fact is that it has become difficult to identify 'the people' in the Church as well as in our political discourse. The twentieth century was the age of the mobilisation of the masses in the nation state as well as in the Church. That age has been replaced by a much more fragmented social and ecclesial body. It used to be easy to identify the Catholic elite with the clergy, Catholic intellectuals, and Catholic political leaders. Now the leadership role of the clergy is in deep trouble, and there are Catholic lay leaders whose voices matter more than many bishops and cardinals together. On the other

---

10. See for example Francis' speech to the bishops during his visit to Mexico, on 13 February 2016 https://w2.vatican.va/content/francesco/it/speeches/2016/february/documents/papa-francesco_20160213_messico-vescovi.html.

hand, 'the people' for the Church is still important but much more as a theological idea (the people of God) than as a homogeneous, socially tangible reality. Fragmented ideologically, socially and ethnically, the globalisation of Catholicism has to deal with the need to redefine who its people are.

One of the unexpected consequences of Vatican II was the beginning of a very profound change of elites in contemporary Catholicism. Understanding the consequences of this is a huge task that runs below the surface of Francis' pontificate. The pope is aware of the change in the elites of the Catholic Church that occurred in the last fifty years more or less. It is interesting to look at the way he addresses two key players in the arena where the battle for Church leadership takes place: the bishops and the new ecclesial movements. Francis addresses bishops in a way that reveals the pope's take on the shortcomings of the "episcopalist" ecclesiology of Vatican II. But the bishops are not the only ones being told about the illusions of their eternal leadership in the Church. Francis' addresses to the Catholic movements (Communion and Liberation, Neocatechumenal Way, etc) always contain the idea that the Church does not need elites that are isolated from the rest of the ecclesial community.

All this tells us that if the theology of the priesthood has not changed in these last fifty years, the very meaning of Church leadership and of the people of the Church have changed significantly. It will suffice here to note the deep and probably irrecoverable crisis of the identification between clergy and Church leadership. The second millennium saw this identification being created beginning with the 'Gregorian revolution' of the eleventh century. The third millennium is probably going to get rid of this identification—partly acknowledging the lived theology of our communities, parly discussing theologically and ecclesiologically the need for a redefinition of Church leadership and ministry.

Centre and Periphery

Vatican II represents a clear step towards a less centralised and an ecclesiologically balanced relationship between the center and the local Churches. The council does so not only in *Lumen Gentium*, but also from the very first document it approved, the liturgical constitution *Sacrosanctum Concilium.*[11] The liturgical constitution stresses the importance of the local Church through the biblical and patristic renewal, which points to the roots of early Christianity as a communion of local communities; through the rediscovery of the Eucharist as the very heart of the Church; through the empowerment of the local bishop as first celebrant within the local Church.

But Vatican II was a first step. This new role of the bishops in the life of local Churches was supported by the final outcome of the liturgical debate, and not by the quite active (later during Vatican II) bishops' lobbying in favor of an institutional *decentralisation* in the global Catholic Church (that is, more autonomy from Rome for the bishops) and *centralisation* in the local church (abolition of the immovability for parish priests, and more control of the religious orders active in the diocese). The same caution is visible in the constitution on the Church *Lumen Gentium*, where chapter III on episcopal collegiality is only an opening towards a different modality of the use of papal primacy, and where collegiality of the bishops is founded on their belonging to the universal *collegium*, and not on their being bishops of a local Church. The Bishops' Synod as it is described in *Christus Dominus* par 5 (following Paul VI's motu proprio *Apostolica Sollicitudo* of September 15, 1965), finally, is not an instrument of decentralization but of important but limited coopting of the bishops by papal power.[12]

On the other hand, the same decree *Christus Dominus* provided the Church with the first groundbreaking text on the episcopal conferences, which Vatican II wanted to become operative in every country.[13] This is where the trajectory towards decentralisation was,

---

11. See Massimo Faggioli, *True Reform: Liturgy and Ecclesiology in Sacrosanctum Concilium* (Collegeville: Liturgical Press 2012).

12. 'Bishops chosen from various parts of the world, in ways and manners established or to be established by the Roman pontiff, render more effective assistance to the supreme pastor of the Church in a deliberative body which will be called by the proper name of Synod of Bishops. Since it shall be acting in the name of the entire Catholic episcopate, it will at the same time show that all the bishops in hierarchical communion partake of the solicitude for the universal Church'. Vatican II, decree *Christus Dominus*, par 5 (28 October 1965), http://www.vatican.va/archive/hist_councils/ii_vatican_council/documents/vat-ii_decree_19651028_christus-dominus_en.html.

13. 'In these days especially bishops frequently are unable to fulfill their office effectively and fruitfully unless they develop a common effort involving

after a promising start during the 1970s, interrupted under John Paul II and Benedict XVI, and where it probably has to resume for the future of the governance of the Church—together with a renewed encouragement from the pope in the contemporary Church that today is difficult to imagine as being temporary.[14]

There is no one key word for the new articulation of the relationship between center and periphery. Collegiality was the buzzword of Vatican II, but the post-Vatican II period learned that it has to be tempered and completed with synodality. The post-Vatican II reforms worked also because they were mandated from a strong universal level. Localism is not necessarily the panacea for what does not work in the governance of the Catholic Church. On the other hand, it is true that in the last three decades the local level has been almost constantly and unnecessarily killed. The manifest humiliation of the prerogatives of the Bishops' conferences (such as in the recent case of the new English translation of the Missal) must be a thing of the past. The excesses of centralisation are clearly part of Francis' experiences with the institutional Church.[15]

Governance for Mission: A Few Proposals

The nineteenth and twentieth centuries have been the golden age for a development of the theology and practice of the papal office and of episcopal ministry. The petrine ministry has changed profoundly between Vatican I and Vatican II, and this change is accelerating with pope Francis. But there are other changes that need to take place in order to re-energise the Catholic Church for the mission of evangelisation: spiritual renewal is necessary, but it cannot be an excuse to delay or to avoid institutional change. This is a time of

---

constant growth in harmony and closeness of ties with other bishops. Episcopal conferences already established in many nations-have furnished outstanding proofs of a more fruitful apostolate. Therefore, this sacred synod considers it to be supremely fitting that everywhere bishops belonging to the same nation or region form an association which would meet at fixed times.' Vatican II, decree *Christus Dominus*, par 37.

14. About the evolution of papal power see Klaus Schatz, *Papal Primacy: From Its Origin to the Present* (Collegeville: Liturgical Press, 1996).
15. See Francis, exhortation *Evangelii Gaudium* (24 November 2013), par 16 and 32.

change for the Catholic Church, also at the institutional level that must correspond to the momentuous changes in the very body of the Church. The global nature of the Church is made more visible by the fact that membership in the Roman Catholic Church today is much more global, less European and less clerical. Therefore it is time to rethink some of the institutions for the government of the Church. The short list of proposals that follows is not complete and is provisional. But it provides a starting point.

The role of *Vatican diplomacy and the nuncios* in their work at the service of the local Churches is just as much in need of a new appraisal in light of the ecclesiology of Vatican II. In particular, the procedures for the bishops' appointments must be changed—at least initially from a symbolic point of view, in the sense of more participation of the local Churches (clergy, lay, and women) who receive a new bishop. This would be in line both with the ancient tradition, with some of the proposals drafted at Vatican II, and with a correct ecclesiology of the local Church. The role of Vatican diplomacy should be maintained, being one of the distinctive elements of the activity of the Catholic Church as a service to the world and to the world Church, in an age where there is a clear need for an authoritative voice speaking on behalf of those who do not have a voice.

The relations between the Roman Curia and *the Bishops' conferences* must change in the sense of a renewed ecclesiology of the local Church. The issues are related to their relationship to the Roman Curia in terms of the representation of the voices of the bishops. It is important to give the Bishops' Conferences power to interact with the Roman Curia collegially as a conference (national or continental). Paradoxically, under Francis it seems that the only call for more activity of the bishops' conferences is coming from the pope and the bishops' conferences are reluctant to take up this invitation.

The Roman Curia must find a balance in the voice of *the Consistory* of cardinals. The issues are the role of the Consistory vis-à-vis the papacy, its composition (who are the members), and the frequency of its meetings. In the midterm it seems possible to leave the Consistory as a tool of the papacy to gauge reactions from the cardinals (many of them being the electoral college of the pope) about particular issues of his choosing, but also on issues brought up by the cardinals. It is important that the Consistory gathers *at least once a year*.

At the local level, *diocesan synods and particular councils* must find a new voice. Diocesan synods and particular councils must be part of a new consideration of the relationship between center and periphery for a reform of the Roman Curia. It is advisable to jump-start the synodal life of the local Churches with some provision requiring the celebration of diocesan synods and particular councils at least every ten years (see Code of Canon Law 1917).

If I Could Advise The Pope

Geraldine Dooge

The Catholic Church does not often take counsel from *The Economist*. But a headline in the lead up to Pope Francis's election would have diverted eyes from the billowing smoke in St Peter's Square. 'Pope, CEO' announced the rationalist's bible, with plenty of advice for the bishops. Why not follow General Electric boss Jeff Immelt's golden rule which is that his firm needed to *disrupt* itself with new ideas from the emerging world, to avoid being displaced by emerging-world rivals?

Cheeky maybe, but the concept of introducing modern corporate discipline to one of the world's oldest institutions is not entirely fanciful and may be wholly appropriate. And redemptive.

The pope is CEO of an all too earthly church as much as he is chief spiritual officer for 1.2 billion Catholics. Yet the Church still operates as if it is the most powerful institution in a settled village structure, instead of a multi-national agency for beliefs, relationships, skills and services, a custodian of moral codes and cultural heritage: the broadest of briefs.

Its facade of secrecy, aloofness and exceptionalism might have persisted if the Church had not breached its trust with the secular world. The sex abuse scandals have blown that compact apart. The scrutiny of the world has become pitiless, as much for the terrible values as for the sheer incompetence on display. The reaction is possibly more than would greet a similar calamity in the private or government sector partly because people had cut the Church such slack over the years.

Today, the wider world is simply disgusted. Many are inclined to ignore the Church's manifold services to society partly because it seems so disinclined to explore why things went awry. Trust must be re-earned in ways the secular world is familiar with. And that means adopting the practices of other big institutions that society has given a license-to-operate, sometimes after big setbacks, like BP, the banks, political parties or like the United States Army after its Vietnam horrors. Now there is an interesting analogy which bears close reflection.

The McKinseys and Boston Consultings of this world are well-used to entering corporate disaster-zones and diagnosing better futures from seemingly impossible messes. I have not served with them. But I have been a Catholic for six decades and have closely studied the institution's innards, its strengths and weaknesses, both as a believer and a reporter. I have also experienced structures within organisations like the organisation I work for (the Australian Broadcasting Corporation—the ABC), which offer intangible goods too, not sacred ones but vital for the community.

So, allow me to appoint myself a temporary consultant to Pope Francis in his role as CEO and let me get to work.

One the of the first messages I would convey would be hard to hear for a seniorcleric,soaccustomedtolegitimacyinheritedovercenturies. The message is it will not be like this from now on. The balance of power has shifted unequivocally between the Church hierarchy and people. That is, recovery really won't be in the pope's hands, or that of his bishops, nomatterhowmuchtheymay sensethehelpofdivineforces.

The Church's future now lies in the hands of the community it should be serving. Just as stars are made-and-unmade by their audience, public perception will be vital. The secular world will choose whether it cares enough for the Church to flourish again, which is both deeply confronting and inviting. Leadership towards this goal is non negotiable.

Having outlined that imperative, I would suggest the prime question facing an incoming CEO of any troubled institution is this: is anything worth saving? Should he consider calling in the (metaphorical) receivers and sell up the properties, paintings and gold crockery?

Certainly, I would expect a new CEO would lament the trashing of the brand wrought by sex scandals, cover-ups, poor management and a structure that owes more to the *ancien regime* than modern practice. Given the tarnished brand, I would expect him to question whether his organisation has the capacity for renewing its moral and spiritual leadership? And whether there is still a viable market for the sort of products offered by the church? What is a reasonable market-share these days anyway?

I would answer the second question first because it has the most compelling answer. Unequivocally, yes: there is a huge demand in the world today for moral and spiritual leadership, for language that cuts through the verbiage and conveys durable meaning. This need is both personal and public.

On the *personal* level, surveys consistently show that most people remain interested in the spiritual life—but not the life of religion. They are actively carving off the religious aspect of the numinous and nurturing the personal/feeling side of belief. They may even have worked hard at excluding religion from their spiritual desires and, some might add, contemporary religious institutions have made it easy for them!

I would submit to a new CEO that surely here is a ready-made market, still available for capture. Here is a brand that can readily mine its rich, established traditions. These answer age-old longings for identity and meaning. They dignify the quest for something deep. Alongside a well-recognised set of rituals, here sits a community offering a language beyond materialism and narcissism—a precious repertoire and not easily found elsewhere.

But the *public* need for religion is just as compelling. For centuries the secular world has drawn on religious principles for its codes of living, its definition of 'a good life'. It still does but is not receiving much fresh input while needing it more than ever. A revolution in technology is exposing the brittleness of modern public codes despite the remarkable advance of our laws. Much wisdom lies untilled in the language of virtue, inherited from the Greeks and tweaked further by the early Christians. Beyond mere lists of commandments, it invites mature contemplation and offers real consolation.

This is surely the job of a good, engaged Church: to articulate what has amounted to a good life over the centuries? How can it be lived now? Various groups offer this product of course. Philosophers Alain de Botton and Michael Sandel, plus copious celebrity psychiatrist authors of self-help books spring to mind. But in terms of potential mass reach and experience, plus that capacity to deliver an incomparable 'extra', or a knock-out drop event, like the recent papal election, the Church should be front-and-centre. Yet it has gone AWOL.

'Despite its disgust, maybe the wider world needs to genuinely consider whether they would like a public world entirely devoid of Church influence', the Pope might say to me. Yes, but the opposite to faith is not atheism, as some sage pointed out recently. It is indifferentism, I would counter. That is the real threat lying within the educated West. It is different within the growth-filled emerging world but rivals there are eating the Church's lunch.

So what of the first question above: does the Church have the capacity to change? Does it have the management, the processes, even the supply chains to deliver new messages to itself, let alone the world?

Sure, the Church has re-invented itself out of some awful stews many times in its history. But as we know, history rhymes not repeats and frankly does not necessarily diagnose exit routes out of current crises.

Ask the United States military after Vietnam, I would remind my pope/CEO. In fact look quite closely there for models. Here was an military that counted three million members at its peak in the mid 1960s, humbled and embarrassed as it was bundled out of a small developing Asian country. Could this lumbering giant really reform itself, the skeptics of the time wondered?

Under the title 'An Army Transformed: The US Army's Post Vietnam Recovery and the Dynamics of Change in Military Organisations', Lieut Col Suzanne Nielsen outlines how it did: (Strategic Studies Institute of the US Army War College in 2010)

> During the 2 decades preceding the Persian Gulf War in 1991, the US Army went through tremendous reform and rejuvenation. First, leaders within military organisations are essential; external developments most often have an indeterminate impact on military change. Second, military reform is about more than changing doctrine. To implement its doctrine, an organisation must have appropriate training practices, personnel policies, organisations, equipment and leader development programs. Third, the implementation of

comprehensive change requires an organisational entity with broad authority to craft, evaluate and execute an integrated program of reforms. Fourth, the process of institutionalising complementary reforms can take several decades. While today's demands differ from those of the past, this report suggests questions that maybe be useful in thinking about change today. The consequences, for good or ill, could be quite significant in terms of resources, lives and the national interest.

And if you, my dear Pope Francis, can not see the obvious parallels with the Church, with its need to supply both style and substance in the service of critical needs, then I might indeed give up hope. Whether or not one approves of the current United States military objectives, the organisation is vastly more relevant than its earlier iteration, regarded as the most effective institution in the country. So could the Church be.

There are other less dramatic examples. Borrowing from international policing experience, the New South Wales Police Force embarked five years ago on a significant programme of cultural change. Under the leadership of Commissioner Andrew Scipione and Assistant Commissioner Catherine Burn the force set itself up to abide by a Customer Service Charter, which they researched meticulously with the community and interpreted very broadly indeed.

Writing in a recent Customer Service Association magazine, the two police executives described, with passion, how they had decided to go beyond just answering the usual complaints about force personnel to addressing root causes.

'The front-line officer needs to understand that 99% (of work) is about the community, only 1% is law enforcement and interaction with actual criminals,' said Assistant Commissioner Burn.

'Why do I see customer service as being important? Because serving customers means investing in the safety and security of communities. And so I see this whole notion of improving customer service as being the driver for us to deliver the leadership that the community right across this state is seeking today,' said Commissioner Scipione.

International best-practice policing, he said, was intensively considering what it called a back-to-basics strategy. And for those who didn't believe this was sufficiently 'hard-edged policing', he disagreed. Itdefinitely prevented crime and above all, set you up well for managing the hard edge, when needed.

Another model is the *New York Times* newspaper which has spent ten tough years recovering from the Jayson Blair disaster, the young reporter who lied, faked and cheated his way through the venerable paper's news room, trashing the brand mightily when discovered. . . by the paper itself. Itled to agonising self-reflection and is clearly still a touchy subject.

'After the scandal and a thorough internal analysis, the *New York Times* management put safeguards in place. One was the role of the public editor. I am the here to give readers a direct place to come to, independent of the *Times*' editing structure, to take complaints about journalistic integrity,' wrote Margaret Sullivan. 'Another reform was the creation of a full-time standards editor, an internal position within the newsroom hierarchy. Still another was a program to thoroughly and regularly evaluate journalists' work.'

The current editor-in-chief Jill Abramson said one of the greatest lessons of the Blair scandal was 'how concerned, hurt and angry our readers were, because this was contrary to everything we stand for— the trust and authenticity that people attach to the *Times*'. Sound familiar?

But there is another clear area of need which is utterly up to the Church to fix, I would tell the Pope: its internal attitudes to staff. Modern management manuals are full of advice to bosses about seriously valuing their staff as their greatest asset. It can be a platitude, obviously. But increasingly, 'well run organisations that battle for good employees are paying much more attention to it. Happy workers do matter because they stay longer, adapt better, self-direct more, don't work-to-rule. Living the good life at work is no longer a joke'.

Yet I've witnessed callousness towards priests and nuns from their own institution that has stunned me. I am afraid I have reluctantly drawn the conclusion that the world beyond the institutional Church, where I live, is a considerably kinder, gentler place by comparison and that it's full of more conscientious ethics and care for its own than the official Church. 'See how those Christians love one another' was the great recruiting tool of the early Christians amidst the harsh Roman world. And the course of history was changed as a result. Time for sometwenty-first century dusting-off.

The management of the Church's human resources (that beige term) will require deep wells of commitment. From the Curia officials down to parish priests, what are the KPI's for these office holders? What is their tenure? Do they even know what their roles should be in a modern world?

Staffing? No organisation would allow its staffing situation to reach a position as dire as that of the Catholic Church. Over half a century, there has been a collapse in the number of priests and nuns available to deliver the Catholic way of life to its 1.2 billion members. Some two thirds of the priests in active parish ministry in Australia, for example are more than sixty years old. Do you know, dear pope, how they are working and driving and managing in this huge country of ours, where the diocese of Toowoomba alone is bigger than France?

A corporate response to this would be urgent recruitment, yes, but it would also look at changing the roles of clergy, bringing in more support staff, streamlining operations.

Women? Did we just raise the question of women's role in the church? It would also look at the training of nuns and priests—those selfless recruits, many of whom entered cloisters when TV came into being and are now living in a Tweeting era.

Ask not what these nuns and priests are delivering to the church but what the church is delivering to these front line troops. A bit of 360 degree evaluation, maybe?

Or take another example: transparency. The corporate world might well have been dragged to the transparency table over the past few decades. But it's embraced the notion vastly more than the Church, which still operates like it's behind a confessional grill.

This culture of secrecy and earthly aloofness was summarised in a *New York Times* article on reforming the Vatican Bank. A European banking official reported that when he pressed for more openness about bank accounts, in line with all other national banking outlets, a Vatican representative shouted: 'How can you ask us such questions?' How can a modern European official, acting on behalf of the public post-GFC, *not* ask?

The third obvious practice that the Church could adopt is accountability. Sister to transparency, accountability lies at the heart of the trust between the promoter of a brand/belief and those who are buying in the store. Much of the community backlash over the abuse crisis could have been avoided had an acknowledged process of accountability been in place. The cover-up is always more destructive than the action: a truth now universally acknowledged in the secular world. And this is surely a good value, not merely shallow spin.

A more prosaic but equally necessary tool of the corporate world is auditing. The idea that an institution of such great wealth is above the need for financial accountability has infected not just the Vatican Bank officials but parish businesses and the many charitable operations of the church.

The regular broad pushes for a review of tax exempt status of church activities indicates that the secular community is no longer willing to accept the word of churches that what they do should be accepted at face value. A few audited accounts may well show these operations deserve tax exemption. Again, the underlying value-base is to be applauded, not suspected.

Admittedly, these principles have been foisted on organisations—often against their will—but they have served them well. Most decent outfits would abhor any reversion to the laissez faire operations or hierarchies of the past, as would their shareholders.

The sad fact is that the corporate world has been delivering on the principles of fairness, kindness, equity, respect, better than the Church: It has outperformed on the element of *caritas*. It has ticked many of the KPIs necessary for the good life. And the Church hasn't.

Could it be time to pick up the phone?

The Pope's Vision for a Renewed Church

Robert Mickens

Pope Francis likes to create discussion, provoke deeper questioning and lead people towards spiritual discernment, a process that requires a good amount of time and patience. It is also a process that can be messy, because that is the reality of any journey through life. The Christian journey is no different. History's first Jesuit pope knows this from his extensive experience of being a pastor in the midst of his people. And now as chief shepherd of the worldwide Church he has continued to encourage people to embrace their messy reality with the courage and trust that comes through faith.

That message is loud and clear in his apostolic exhortation on marriage and the family, *Amoris Laetitia* (19 March 2019). In that text Pope Francis has proposed a clear vision of Christian discipleship. It is one based more on personal responsibility and prayerful discernment than on the mere following of church rules.

In this same document he has sketched a profile of the ordained minister. Both priests and bishops are to be servant-leaders characterised by mercy and patience. They are to humbly accompany, dialogue and collaborate with their people as fellow disciples. The pope doesn't want pastors haranguing Catholics who fall short of the mark with rules and moral laws 'as if they were stones to throw at people's lives'.

In essence, he has re-proposed the model of discipleship and servant-leadership that emerged from the Second Vatican Council (1962–65). And in doing so, it is as if he's re-started the journey that the Church had embarked upon in the first decade or so following Vatican II. John Paul II halted that journey early on in his long pontificate (1978–2005) and then began to 'correct' and recalibrate it.

No one who has been closely following Pope Francis since his pontificate dramatically began on the evening of 13 March 2013 should be greatly surprised by the model of discipleship and leadership he offers in *Amoris Laetitia*. It is, in a sense, just one more elaboration of all that he has been trying to embody and proclaim during his ministry as Bishop of Rome.

His first really clear articulation of his vision for the Church came in a blockbuster interview published in September 2013 in the Italian journal, *La Civiltà Cattolica*. The periodical's editor, Fr Antonio Spadaro SJ, spent several hours conversing with the pope and the transcript of their exchange has provided readers with an even better understanding of the man who, in only a few months after his election to the papacy, had already begun endearing himself to people around the world. Significantly, the interview was simultaneously released in multiple languages in other Jesuit publications around the globe.

During their exchange Fr Spadaro pointed out that many Catholics had high hopes for Church reform, especially at the Vatican. But the Jesuit Pope issued a word of caution that perhaps too many people ignored at the time. He said concrete reforms would probably not happen too quickly. 'I am always wary of decisions made hastily,' he said. 'Many think that changes and reforms can take place in a short time,' he added. But noting that 'discernment takes time', he said: 'I believe that we always need time to lay the foundations for real, effective change.'

And time is an extremely important notion in Pope Francis' thinking and approach to life and governance. He has said on many occasions that 'time is greater than space'. He explained that most clearly in his 2013 apostolic exhortation, *Evangelii Gaudium* (EG) or 'Joy of the Gospel'.

Progress in building a people in peace, justice and fraternity depends on four principles related to constant tensions present in every social reality,' Pope Francis points out in this extremely insightful text (cf EG, 217–237).

Here are the four principles:

1. Time is greater than space
2. Unity prevails over conflict
3. Realities are more important than ideas

4.   The whole is great than the sum of the parts

Note that Francis says these are related to tensions in '*every* social reality'. And while he does not say it specifically, that would also include the reality of the Church. This becomes evident in the way he explains how these principles 'can guide the development of life in society and the building of a people where differences are harmonized within a shared pursuit'. Indeed, the Catholic Church is characterized more and more by divisions and tensions that stem from different ideologies and points of view. Pope Francis has tried to harmonize these differences within his global faith community and he as followed the four principles cited above to do so. They undergird his method of engaging in ecclesial governance, international peacemaking and prophetic pastoral service.

Time is Greater than Space

'A constant tension exists between fullness and limitation,' Francis writes in EG. 'People live poised between each individual moment and the greater, brighter horizon of the utopian future as the final cause which draws us to itself,' he says. The pope believes the notion that time is greater than space is 'a first principle for progress in building a people'. It is one that 'enables us to work slowly but surely, without being obsessed with immediate results'. It is a principle that 'helps us patiently to endure difficult and adverse situations, or inevitable changes in our plans' and 'invites us to accept the tension between fullness and limitation, and to give a priority to time' and processes.

The opposite of this—where 'spaces and power are preferred to time and processes'—'means madly attempting to keep everything together in the present, trying to possess all the spaces of power and of self-assertion' which can only 'crystallize processes and presume to hold them back'.

Those who have grown impatient with the seemingly slow pace of reform in the Church and at the Vatican, have paid too little attention to what the pope writes in *Evangelii Gaudium.*

> Giving priority to time means being concerned about initiating processes rather than possessing spaces. Time governs spaces, illumines them and makes them links in a

constantly expanding chain, with no possibility of return. What we need, then, is to give priority to actions which generate new processes in society and engage other persons and groups who can develop them to the point where they bear fruit in significant historical events. Without anxiety, but with clear convictions and tenacity (EG, 223)

Pope Francis says 'immediate results that yield easy, quick short-term political gains' do not, in the end, 'enhance human fullness'. And here he quotes the late Italian-German theologian and priest, Roman Guardini: 'The only measure for properly evaluating an age is to ask to what extent it fosters the development and attainment of a full and authentically meaningful human existence, in accordance with the peculiar character and the capacities of that age.'

The pope says this is not just a way to gauge the health and development of society.

This criterion also applies to evangelization, which calls for attention to the bigger picture, openness to suitable processes and concern for the long run. The Lord himself, during his earthly life, often warned his disciples that there were things they could not yet understand and that they would have to await the Holy Spirit (cf Jn 16:12–13). The parable of the weeds among the wheat (cf Mt 13:24–30) graphically illustrates an important aspect of evangelization: the enemy can intrude upon the kingdom and sow harm, but ultimately he is defeated by the goodness of the wheat (EG, 224).

The principle that time is greater than space has become fundamental to understanding Pope Francis' efforts to renew the Church and reform some of its structures, such as its central bureaucracy (the Roman Curia).

Evangelii Gaudium: The Program of the Pontificate, a Blueprint for Renewal

Evangelii Gaudium appeared just a few months after the publication of his long interview in *La Civiltà Cattolica* and the other Jesuit journals. And one gains a fuller insight into the Francis' thoughts by reading the two texts together. The exhortation, which came out in November 2013, was the first major document of his fledgling pontificate. (He had issued an encyclical some months earlier, but it was an inherited document prepared almost entirely by Benedict XVI.) It is not all together clear why the Jesuit pope issued the 48,000-word text in the form of an apostolic exhortation rather than in the more lofty classification of an encyclical letter, but he has since told his closest aides that he considers EG the most important document of his pontificate. In fact, it offers a programmatic outline for his ministry as Bishop of Rome and illustrates, in broad strokes, a vision for Church renewal and reform.

The Jesuit pope says in the first pages of this refreshingly forward-looking document that it is based on the teaching of the Second Vatican Council's constitution on the Church, *Lumen Gentium*. He says it offers 'guidelines' for a 'new phase of evangelization'. It not only calls for reforming Church structures and attitudes, but it also critiques elements that hinder the spread of the Gospel. These include a 'trickle-down' economic model based on a 'deified market' that hurt the poor; 'veritable attacks on religious freedom or a new persecution directed against Christians'; an 'unwelcoming atmosphere' in Catholic communities; the exclusion of the laity in 'decision-making' because of 'excessive clericalism'; the presence of cliques, factions and 'veritable witch hunts' inside the Church; and Catholics who have an 'ostentatious preoccupation for the liturgy, for doctrine and the Church's prestige', rather than preaching the main message of God's love and mercy towards all people.

'Pastoral ministry in a missionary style is not obsessed with the disjointed transmission of a multitude of doctrines to be insistently imposed,' the pope warns. He then criticizes the Church for holding on to a language and formulations that are sometimes 'alien' to people's understanding or way of speaking. He also says there is a need to 're-examine' certain Church laws, precepts and customs—even those that are 'beautiful' or have 'deep historic roots'—if they no longer communicate the Gospel or have 'the same usefulness for directing and shaping peoples lives'.

In one of the most striking passages, the pope says the Church must not close its doors, including those of the sacraments, to anyone. 'The Eucharist, although it is the fullness of sacramental life, is not a prize for the perfect but a powerful medicine and nourishment for the weak,' he notes. He urges 'prudence and boldness' in reflecting on the 'pastoral consequences' of this principle.

Francis again affirms his preference for a 'poor Church that is poor' and one that is 'bruised, hurting and dirty because it has been out on the streets', rather than one locked up and safe. 'More than fear of going astray, my hope is that we will be moved by the fear of being shut up within structures that give a false sense of security, within rules that make us harsh judges, within habits which make us feel safe, while at our doors people are starving and Jesus does not tire of saying to us: 'Give them something to eat' (Mk 6:37),' he writes.

Francis says EG 'has a programmatic significance and important consequences' that are aimed at provoking a 'pastoral and missionary conversion which cannot leave things as they presently are'. He makes clear that he expects 'everyone to apply the guidelines of this document generously and courageously, without inhibition or fear'.

Synod of Bishops: Vehicle for Church Reform

The Jesuit pope also declared early on that he wanted to revamp the Synod of Bishops, strip the Roman Curia of the 'censorship' power it has often wielded over bishops and episcopal conferences and re-think the way the Bishop of Rome exercises 'primacy' in the Church.

'Maybe it is time to change the methods of the Synod of Bishops, because it seems to me that the current method is not dynamic,' the pope said in that first major interview with the Jesuit publications. And change it he has!

Having attended a few Synod assemblies in the past while still a bishop in Buenos Aires, he knew that many bishops hedge their bets. They don't always say what they really think when speaking in front of the pope. Instead, they say what they think he and his collaborators in the Curia want to hear.

That's why Francis felt it was necessary on the very first working day of the 2014 Synod assembly to do what none of his predecessors had ever done before—he instructed the bishops (that is, gave them permission) to speak frankly, openly and with boldness. 'You must say everything you feel with parrhesia,' he said, using the Greek word for speaking up without fear. The message was clear. He wanted the bishops to say what was really on their minds, but he also told them to listen respectfully to one another.

Why is this important? Because, as we see in *Evangelii Gaudium*, Francis does not 'believe that the papal magisterium should be expected to offer a definitive or complete word on every question which affects the Church and the world.' It is 'not advisable' for the pope and his Rome-based collaborators to 'take the place of local bishops in the discernment of every issue which arises in their territory', he notes. 'I am conscious of the need to promote a sound 'decentralization', he says. And, to put on exclamation point on it, he declares: 'Excessive centralization, rather than proving helpful, complicates the Church's life and her missionary outreach.'

As I have argued before, the best chance for carrying out a sound or healthy decentralization, it would seem, is by giving greater authority to episcopal conferences and the Synod of Bishops. A third institution that could also be reformed with the aim of decentralizing decision-making away from Rome is the office of metropolitan archbishops. Since the Council of Trent (1545–1563) juridical authority that once was constituent of the metropolitans has all but disappeared, leaving them with only the strange woolen band that is draped over their shoulders and precedence in liturgical processions. These, and their title, are basically the only things that differentiate them from other bishops.

Enhancing the role of these three institutions, as well as utilizing his Council of Cardinals (C9) are the best ways for reforming the Curia through the necessary decentralization for which the great Jesuit canon lawyer and theologian, Fr Ladislas Orsy, has long been a leading advocate.

The pope has already shown his seriousness about bolstering the Synod, of which he—like patriarchs in the Eastern Churches—is the head or president. Since Paul VI resurrected this ancient body (or at least a form of it) in 1965, no pope has ever taken this role so seriously or been so directly involved in its Synod's governance.

First, Francis decided to call the Synod into session twice over the course of twelve months (October 2014 and October 2015) to discuss issues surrounding marriage and the family. But several months before the bishops even came to Rome he had the Synod secretariat send a questionnaire to all bishops of the world, asking them to canvass the views of their priests and people. This unprecedented survey then became the draft document for the first autumn session of the Synod in 2014.

What most people continue to fail to see is that this methodology was not principally about coming to ultimate decisions on thorny questions facing the Church's doctrine and/or pastoral practice regarding marriage, family and human sexuality.

It was about initiating a process—one that would, hopefully, begin changing the mentality of Catholics; first, those who wear the hats of authority and, then, those in the pulpit and the pew. Currently, this is a work in progress and, for many reasons, likely always will be.

But there are some concrete and even juridical moves Francis could initiate to strengthen the Synod of Bishops as a means of balancing the Church's sill overly impoverished and highly centralised (that is Romanised) ecclesiology. The popes from Paul VI onwards have consigned their authority over the Synod to delegated presidents. Francis has continued the practice when the Synod holds its general assemblies, but perhaps he should re-think that and begin exercising his presidency—without such delegates—during these gatherings, too.

This would strengthen the sense of collegiality by immersing the Bishop of Rome more fully into the sessions as an active participant, rather than a type of hallowed figure who hovers over them. Such a shift would also lead, of necessity, to conferring decision-making authority to the Synod and promoting the collegiality of all bishops acting 'cum et sub' (with and under the authority of) the Successor of Peter. Paul VI's 1965 'motu proprio' establishing the Synod, *Apostolica Sollicitudo,* makes it clear that this body can 'enjoy the power of making decisions when such power is conferred upon it by the Roman Pontiff; in this case, it belongs to him to ratify the decisions of the Synod'.

Will Pope Francis take this decisive step? It is still not clear. But in a major address in October 2015 to mark the fiftieth anniversary of the establishment of the Synod of Bishops he made it clear that further developments to this permanent body would necessarily effect the role of the Roman Pontiff.

'I am persuaded that in a synodal Church, greater light can be shed on the exercise of the Petrine primacy. The pope is not, by himself, above the Church; but within it as one of the baptised, and within the college of bishops as a bishop among bishops, called at the same time—as Successor of Peter—to lead the Church of Rome which presides in charity over all the Churches,' he said.

He spoke of the need for an 'inverted pyramid', which would turn the clericalist model of Church completely on its head, put what is currently at the top (bishops) below what is currently the base (the people). This obviously unsettled those who were already made nervous by his vision of 'a synodal Church' in which 'priests and laity are called to cooperate with the bishop'; where the hierarchy (clergy), through 'listening and sharing', must 'keep connected to the 'base' and start from people and their daily problems'.

The Synod of Bishops, the Pope said, is 'only the most evident manifestation of a dynamism of communion which inspires all ecclesial decisions'. That dynamism is synodality—praying, discussing, discerning and walking together—at every level of the Church. It is just too radical a vision for those clericalists (both among the laity and the clergy) who are troubled by Pope Francis and the style of Church he is trying to bring to birth.

However, others have been energized by this new emphasis. The process of synodality (not just within the Synod of Bishop itself, but involving all the baptised) and the way it has unfolded from late 2013 up to the present has caught the attention of a vast majority of people who consider themselves members of the Church and many others who are outside the Church's boundaries. That's because, due to his own genius or God's providence, Pope Francis chose a topic that lent itself to piquing the interests and stoking the passions of just about everyone on the planet.

Had he decided that the Synod of Bishops should focus on Church governance—papal primacy, episcopal collegiality, subsidiarity and synodality at all levels—most people would have yawned. But by choosing the 'family' as the topic he, in fact, thrust the entire Church (and those who consider themselves un-churched, yet interested bystanders) into a lived experience of synodality.

Those with clear eyes have seen this. 'For me personally, one real fruit of the Synod has been a deeper and richer understanding of synodality in the life of the Church,' said Archbishop Mark Coleridge of Brisbane (Australia) who emerged during the 2015 Synod session as one of the most earnest supporters of Francis's project. 'Another thing now clear is that the work of the Synod won't be finished by Saturday evening once we've voted on the final document. The journey will continue, as it must,' the archbishop said as that gathering was drawing to an end.

In his 2013 interview with *Civiltà Cattolica* the pope emphasised that synodality must be reinforced at 'the various levels' of the Church and suggested that this may well require more collaboration and consultation with leaders of the Orthodox Churches. 'From them we can learn more about the meaning of episcopal collegiality and the tradition of synodality,' he said. And he voiced an openness to efforts to recovering the way the 'church was governed in the early centuries, before the breakup of East and West'.

It is still too early to say whether Francis will succeed in spreading synodality at all levels of the Church. Or whether he is able to forge greater cooperation with the Orthodox. But there are dioceses and national episcopal conferences around the world that have shown a willingness to embrace a more synodal model. And Francis took a major step towards smoothing out relations with the Orthodox in September 2015 when he held an historic meeting with Patriarch of Moscow and All Russia. It took place in Cuba as the pope was making his way to the United States for his first-ever visit to North America's dominant country.

The pope's willingness to meet to meet the patriarch without setting any preconditions was strongly criticized by Byzantine Catholics in Ukraine who have felt persecuted by the Russian Orthodox Church. That criticism was not unlike the strong voices of more doctrinally conservative bishops during the two-year Synod process on marriage and the family. In both cases, the charge was that the pope risked betraying the faith by giving a platform to conflicting voices. But Francis did not create the conflict; he merely recognized it. And he did what he's been doing with all situations and issues that at first appear irreconcilable—he confronted it. This is the second principle he cites in *Evangelii Gaudium* for dealing with tensions in a group or society.

Unity Prevails Over Conflict

'Conflict cannot be ignored or concealed. It has to be faced,' he says. 'But if we remain trapped in conflict, we lose our perspective, our horizons shrink and reality itself begins to fall apart. In the midst of conflict, we lose our sense of the profound unity of reality,' he wisely notes.

Francis says there are two ways people often deal with conflict and neither is constructive. There are those 'simply look at it and go their way as if nothing happened; they wash their hands of it and get on with their lives'. While 'others embrace it in such a way that they become its prisoners; they lose their bearings, project onto institutions their own confusion and dissatisfaction and thus make unity impossible'. Instead, he proposes a 'third way'—'the willingness to face conflict head on, to resolve it and to make it a link in the chain of a new process' (cf EG, 227)

The pope believes people can 'build communion amid disagreement' if they 'are willing to go beyond the surface of the conflict and to see others in their deepest dignity'. This is predicated on the principle that unity is greater than conflict and it opens up the possibility of achieving 'a diversified and life-giving unity'. He writes: 'This is not to opt for a kind of syncretism, or for the absorption of one into the other, but rather for a resolution which takes place on a higher plane and preserves what is valid and useful on both sides.' (cf EG, 228).

According to Francis, 'unity is greater than conflict' is a Gospel principle based on Christ reconciling all things and making them one—in peace—in himself

> The message of peace is not about a negotiated settlement but rather the conviction that the unity brought by the Spirit can harmonize every diversity. It overcomes every conflict by creating a new and promising synthesis. Diversity is a beautiful thing when it can constantly enter into a process of reconciliation and seal a sort of cultural covenant resulting in a 'reconciled diversity' (EG, 230).

The Attitude Adjustment Program and the Roman Curia

The cardinal-electors at the last conclave gave Pope Francis a clear mandate to reform the Roman Curia, especially to clean up financial improprieties and corrupt management practices. And, on numerous occasions during his first weeks and months in office, the new pope gave every indication that he would prefer closing down the so-called 'Vatican Bank' and other bank-like offices run by the Holy See. But opposition to that plan was too fierce. So Francis chose Australian Cardinal George Pell, a conservative pragmatist with a reputation for running over anyone who gets in his way, to oversee a financial reform of these Vatican institutions.

While most of the media have made financial reform the litmus test of this pontificate's success or failure, the pope has been more focused on changing the mentality and ethos inside the Catholic Church, just as he spelled out in *Evangelii Gaudium*. In fact, he said from the very beginning of his pontificate that the first and most essential reform must be a change of mentality. 'The structural and organizational reforms are secondary—that is, they come afterward,' he said in that seminal interview in *La Civiltà Cattolica*. And for the pope the 'attitude adjustment program', as I like to call it, must take effect, first of all, among the Church's ministers. He says they should not be acting 'like bureaucrats or government officials' but as 'people who can warm the hearts of the people'.

Over the past three years, this 'conversion', if you will, has been slow in coming. But there are new signs everyday that it is more firmly taking root. And this is serving to prepare (or soften up) the entire Church for the concrete changes that will eventually come. But it has been an uphill battle to effect the change of ethos of the Roman Curia, especially among its most reluctant and resistant bureaucrats. The elimination or merging of Vatican offices will make no significant difference if the 'curialist' mentality is not severely curbed and corrected.

Consider this: Francis is the first pope in more than a century, dating back to St Pius X (1835–1914), who has never studied or worked in the Eternal City. He is an outsider who cannot rely on old Roman friendships or alliance, which would normally be an advantage in navigating the treacherous waters that can sometimes gush through the headquarters of the Holy See. He is also the first pope in history to have served as president of a national episcopal conference. [Note: today's conferences only began to take shape in the late nineteenth and early twentieth centuries.] As conference president, and also as a cardinal archbishop heading a major diocese, he has experienced, first-hand, the obstruction, lack of cooperation and attitude of superiority that some curia heads have used to keep local bishops in check. As the late English Cardinal Basil Hume said, 'They treat us like school boys!'

So how can he move against this?

First, he could adopt the clear principle of separating the executive office from the managing office. The Bishop of Rome and other diocesan bishops (in their local Churches and in episcopal conferences) are the executives. Heads and officials of Roman Curia offices are managers. They work for the pope and the local bishops, not the other way around. A big part of this is respecting the rightful autonomy and authority of local bishops, that they are employed to serve and assist. In his reform plan Pope Francis reportedly insisted that Rome must do better in this regard.

Second, he could implement protocols that will help curtail clerical 'careerism.' One way to do this is by sticking to the five-year term limits, in all but a few exceptions. He has already stopped granting the title of 'monsignor' to diocesan priests under the age of sixty-five. He should override the opposition and apply this same rule to those priests working in the Roman Curia and the diplomatic corps. And, it bears repeating, it would be better if someone appointed to head a Vatican office did not automatically become a bishop or a cardinal.

While he and his C9 advisory group slowly ponder plans for restructuring the curia, Francis, it seems, has largely circumvented or neutralized those Vatican offices that are not being useful or fully cooperative in promoting his overall vision for Church renewal (especially the lavishly merciful and accident-prone version of it).

The Congregation for the Doctrine of the Faith (CDF) is a case in point. In the three years that Francis has been Bishop of Rome the doctrinal congregation has not issued a single major document to the global Church. Its first text—a minor 'letter' on the relationship between bishops and new ecclesial movements—did not come out until June 2016. In previous pontificates the CDF would routinely publish two to four documents every year, sometimes even more. The last one came in April 2012. It was the Doctrinal Assessment of the Leadership Conference of Women Religious (LCWR) in the United States. Significantly, Francis brought the so-called 'investigation' of the LCWR to a quiet and peaceful end in the second year of his pontificate, effectively halting the doctrinal department's last major undertaking.

Pope Francis simply has not placed great importance on the work of the CDF prefect, Cardinal Gerhard Müller, or his department in way that John Paul II or Benedict XVI did. On the contrary, Francis has circumvented the German cardinal and has virtually emptied his office of any real power, authority or utility in his pontificate. The pope has not asked the prefect to officially present his writings or initiatives, except for the July 2013 encyclical, *Lumen Fidei*, which was actually the work of Benedict XVI.

Rather, the pope has relied heavily on theological help from 'the ends of the earth', as he would put it. It is pretty well established that his primary ghostwriter is Archbishop Victor Manuel Fernandez, rector of the Catholic University of Argentina in Buenos Aires. And he has shown his high regard for and reliance on the thinking of Cardinal Walter Kasper since the first days of his pontificate. Fr Antonio Spadaro of *La Civiltà Cattolica* is also known to be one of a handful of Jesuits in Rome that he consults and relies on for information.

Establishing or strengthening structures that will facilitate a more synodal Church and reforming the Roman Curia are important for the long-term (time is greater than space). But many people feel the pope must take urgent action to change the hierarchy, appointing bishops and creating cardinals that are fully committed to his vision for the Church—especially that which he sets forth in *Evangelii Gaudium* and *Amoris Laetitiae*.

Shaping the College of Cardinals

Pope Francis can immediately put his stamp on the Church's leadership and direction by his selection of new cardinals under the age of 80, those eligible to vote in a conclave—the ones that will eventually elect his successor. The only problem is that if he follows the current legislation (set by Paul VI) he will not have many opportunities to give out the red hat. That's because there is a ceiling of 120 electors. John

Paul II dispensed with this rule at times, which was his right. That's because the College of Cardinals is a human-invented institution. It is not part of the ancient Church's structure and, more importantly, it is not part of the sacrament of Holy Orders, although John XXIII decreed that newly named cardinals who are not already bishops are be ordained to the episcopate. And John's rule, just like Paul's, has also been waved on occasion.

If Francis adheres to the 120 ceiling of electors he would, through natural attrition, he will have only twenty-four slots to fill over the next three years. Add that to the 31 electors he's named up to now and it is obvious that his personally chosen cardinals will still not form a majority of voters even at the end of 2018. There is no guarantee—in fact, it is doubtful—that the current make-up of the electing body would choose a new pope similar to Francis or eager to continue the renewal and reforms he has painstakingly begun.

There are a couple of ways around this seeming conundrum. Since the College of Cardinals has not always existed and has not always been the body that elected the pope, Francis could modify its functions or disband it. Paul VI briefly contemplated a drastic reform of the method of papal election that included the presidents of episcopal conferences and voting delegates from other sectors of the Church. Such a change has strong merits, but it would create a huge backlash from many Catholics. And it would not be advisable for an elderly pope to take on the herculean task of such a monumental and controversial reform.

The more logical and pragmatic course would be to raise the limit on the number of electors (which is arbitrary anyway) from the current 120 to, say, 140 or 150. In a global Church that the Vatican boasts is growing, this would be normal and reasonable.

Urgently Needed: A New Model for Appointing Bishops

The felicitous flowering of decentralization, synodality and episcopal collegiality will be predicated on improving the quality of bishops. Unfortunately, it will probably take two or three generations before we will see a perceptible change in this area. And that is only if the successor(s) of Pope Francis continue to make this type of reform a priority. In the meantime, the current pope has another urgent task—finding a new way to select good bishops.

Already back in February 2014, in an unusually lengthy address, he told members of the Congregation for Bishops they need to do a better job in finding new candidates to head dioceses around the world. 'The Church does not need apologists of personal causes or crusaders of personal battles, but humble and trusting sewers of the truth… men who are patient because they know the weeds will never be so many to overtake the field,' he said.

The pope said bishops should 'safeguard doctrine, not by measuring the world's distance from the truth it contains, but by fascinating the world, enchanting it with the beauty of love, and seducing it' with the freedom that the Gospel offers. He said bishops must be 'courageous' enough to intercede for their people the same way Abraham begged God not to destroy the people of Sodom and Gomorrah. 'A man who does not have the courage to argue with God on behalf of his people cannot be a bishop,' he said, scandalizing some. 'I say this with all my heart, I am convinced,' he ad-libbed.

Francis said the selection of bishops should not be determined by the will of 'factions, cliques or hegemonies' among those involved in vetting candidates. He said he was 'certain' good future bishops existed, but 'maybe we are not going around the fields enough to search for them'.

The problem lies only partly with the Congregation for Bishops. The deeper and more controversial question is whether an office in Rome—or, indeed, the Bishop of Rome—should be appointing bishops in other territories. It was not always thus. Up until the thirteenth century papal intervention in the local election of bishops (or their appointment by monarchs) was very rare. From that point onwards, though, the Bishop of Rome began to become increasingly more involved by claiming the right of *confirmation* of any bishops' election. The Council of Trent (1545–1563) confirmed the pope's authority over the entire Church throughout the world and his right to *approve* the election or appointment of bishops. Then in 1870 with the First Vatican Council and the declaration of papal infallibility, the Bishop of Rome's full and absolute power over the entire Church was dogmatized and, from then onwards, he began appointing bishops.

In the current system the apostolic nuncio plays the most crucial role. He is supposed to make discreet inquiries among a representation of the diocesan clergy and respected lay people when he draws up the terna (or three names) of candidates that he submits to Rome. It is an extremely subjective and arbitrary process, very much influenced by an old-boys' network of current bishops that tends to act as a self-preservation dynasty by promoting their protégés and friends to the episcopacy. Cardinals, especially those who are members of the Congregation for Bishops, are fundamental in pushing forward a candidate—especially for promotion to major posts. In practice, members of the congregation meet to vote on the three names that the nuncio presents and then they are given to the pope to choose one.

But how many priests and other baptised faithful have a significant voice in the appointment of bishops, especially those to the most important dioceses and major sees? Are their concerns listened to seriously? This is not to say that the 'election' of bishops (that's what the Holy See calls such appointments, underlining the more ancient practice) should be done by widespread popular vote. That, in all likelihood, would be a recipe for disaster. But there should be a more serious process that involves a significant representation of the entire community in identifying the most qualified and gifted leaders. And it should be the rule, not the exception, that the choice (or recommendation) of candidate generally be from the local clergy, especially in long-established dioceses. Such an 'election process' could be re-established, albeit with provisions for changed modern-day situations, because while it is true that the Church is not democracy, neither is it an oligarchy.

Pope Francis and his cardinal advisors (C9) have discussed the issue of selecting bishops, though it has not been reported what— if anything—they have proposed so far as possible changes are considered. Some have criticised the pope for having frequently rejected the candidates that are presented to him by the prefect of the Congregation for Bishops—currently Cardinal Marc Ouellet—and then choosing someone who is not even on the terna. But he has not been very quick about it. Obviously the nuncios and the congregation are not supplying candidates he is eager to approve.

The Decline—In number and quality—of Priests

The vocations shortage has become an acute crisis almost everywhere except, perhaps, in Africa. But the situation is uneven there, too. The Argentine Pope knows there is a serious problem, yet he has insisted that even worse than ordaining too few priests is ordaining bad ones. On a number of occasions he has criticized bishops and religious communities for accepting candidates that are unbalanced or have been 'expelled from other seminaries', and then trying to justify this irresponsible decision with the excuse that 'they need priests'.

It has long been argued that there is no lack of talented, dedicated and holy candidates that God is calling forth to serve the People of God in the ordained ministry. The problem is that the criteria the Catholic hierarchy has for selecting future priests ('only celibate males need apply') eliminates so many of the best candidates.

A bishop from Brazil has gone on record as saying that Pope Francis, apparently like Paul VI before him, would be open to ordaining married men if the bishops' conference of a particular country or international region were to endorse such a plan. But not many bishops over the past twenty-five years or so have spoken out publicly in favor of married priests; certainly not the ambitious among them, since they knew that if they did so in the previous two pontificates they could kiss any possibility of career advancement goodbye.

In paragraph 42 of *Evangelii Gaudium* the Pope writes:

> In her ongoing discernment, the Church can also come to see that certain customs not directly connected to the heart of the Gospel, even some which have deep historical roots, are no longer properly understood and appreciated. Some of these customs may be beautiful, but they no longer serve as means of communicating the Gospel. We should not be afraid to re-examine them.

This could be applied to law of celibacy for ordained priests of the Latin Rite. It has deep historical roots and may be beautiful. But the same goes for the married priesthood, which has always been maintained even, if limitedly, in the Roman Church.

It is impossible to argue convincingly that prohibiting married men from the priesthood is directly connected to the Gospel. But at a closed-door meeting with the Italian bishops in May 2106 one visibly nervous prelate asked Francis about talk that he is open to a married priesthood. 'Priestly celibacy remains as it is,' the pope allegedly said in reply. It is an interesting response that most people interpreted as meaning 'the celibate priesthood remains as it is'. But that is not what he said. Priestly celibacy could very well continue even alongside a married clergy. In fact, it already does, though under extraordinary circumstance.

Some of the more reform-minded bishops—mostly those who are already retired—believe the election of Francis offers hope for greater movement on the issue. One of the them—Crispian Hollis, the Bishop-emeritus of Portmouth, England—has written: 'This is surely the logical step forward and I find this increasingly to be the 'mind of the Church', at least in those parishes where I am pastorally engaged.'

There are also other bishops still heading dioceses who have also spoken up for such a development, but they are very few in number.

The Holy People of God

Unfortunately, the biggest resistance to the change of ethos and vision of Church that Pope Francis is trying to effect comes from bishops and the priests who have been ordained within the past fifteen or twenty years. There is no indication the Francis has attracted candidates to seminary that are markedly different from the most recent generation seminarians (and now priests) who, inspired by the more traditional style and mentality in vogue in the previous pontificate, are more focused on the cultic and celebratory aspects of the priesthood than on the servant-leadership, smell of the sheep model the Francis is proposing.

But the baptised faithful, in overwhelming numbers, seem to be on board with direction in which the pope is trying to nudge the Church. It is a Church that is not preoccupied with the insular confines of the sanctuary or sacristy, but one that is freed from the weight of its plaster statues and clerical costumes to carry the Gospel out of pious spaces and into the into the messiness of the world.

It is a Church where realities are more important than ideas. 'This calls for rejecting the various means of masking reality: angelic forms of purity, dictatorships of relativism, empty rhetoric, objectives more ideal than real, brands of ahistorical fundamentalism, ethical systems bereft of kindness, intellectual discourse bereft of wisdom,' Francis says in *Evangelii Gaudium* (No 231).

> We have politicians—and even religious leaders—who wonder why people do not understand and follow them, since their proposals are so clear and logical. Perhaps it is because they are stuck in the realm of pure ideas and end up reducing politics or faith to rhetoric. Others have left simplicity behind and have imported a rationality foreign to most people (EG, 232).

The pope says this third principle related to tensions in society is rooted in 'the incarnation of the word and its being put into practice'.

> The principle of reality, of a word already made flesh and constantly striving to take flesh anew, is essential to evangelization. It helps us to see that the Church's history is a history of salvation, to be mindful of those saints who inculturated the Gospel in the life of our peoples and to reap the fruits of the Church's rich bimillennial tradition, without pretending to come up with a system of thought detached from this treasury, as if we wanted to reinvent the Gospel. At the same time, this principle impels us to put the word into practice, to perform works of justice and charity which make that word fruitful. Not to put the word into practice, not to make it reality, is to build on sand, to remain in the realm of pure ideas and to end up in a lifeless and unfruitful self-centredness and Gnosticism (EG, 233).

Nowhere does Pope Francis demonstrate concretely what he means when he says reality is greater than ideas than in his pastoral approach to people. There are no categories, there are no issues. There are only persons. And real, individual human beings do not fit easily not ideal boxes. The apostolic letter, *Amoris Laetitiae*, spells out in black and white that not everything *is* black and white, especially when it comes to rules, regulations and all Church teaching.

'I understand those who prefer a more rigorous pastoral care which leaves no room for confusion,' he writes. 'But I sincerely believe that Jesus wants a Church attentive to the goodness which the Holy Spirit sows in the midst of human weakness, a Mother who, while clearly expressing her objective teaching, 'always does what good she can, even if in the process, her shoes get soiled by the mud of the street', he says.

The bottom line is that Francis acknowledges that we all fall short of the Christian ideal. Every single one of us. That is why he can say with all sincerity, 'I am a sinner.' And that is why we are invited to join him in saying, with the greatest humility and compassion, 'Who am I to judge?'

A Final Thought: The Tolerant, Inclusive and Merciful Pastor

It has only been a few years since Pope Francis was elected Bishop of Rome. And so much has happened that is hard to believe it has been such a relatively short period of time. He took up his ministry in a deeply divided Church, one that still is fractured. But it seems that ever so gradually the walls of separation in this giant household of faith are slowly dissolving like sand in an hourglass. It is true that his prophetic words, simple gestures and jettisoning of protocol have appealed more to so-called Vatican II, reform-minded or social justice Catholics than to devotees of the Tridentine Mass or the strict interpretation of doctrine. On the other hand, there is an 'old fashionedness' about him—like his deep and sincere sense of traditional piety, insistence on going to confession and his talk of the devil—that reassures those of a more traditional Catholicism. Even the head of the still schismatic Society of St Pius X (the 'Lefevbrists') has marveled at the human and spiritual qualities of Francis and his willingness to encounter others, to listen to them and to empathize with them.

This pope is not a progressive. He is not a traditionalist. He is not conservative or liberal. He is evangelical and merciful and inclusive. He wants a Church that will embrace everyone, especially those furthest afield, those on the margins. He believes that the whole is greater than the sum of its parts and that, like a polyhedron, all the parts can converge while preserving their distinctiveness (cf EG, 235, 236).

> Pastoral and political activity alike seek to gather in this polyhedron the best of each. There is a place for the poor and their culture, their aspirations and their potential. Even people who can be considered dubious on account of their errors have something to offer which must not be overlooked. It is the convergence of peoples who, within the universal order, maintain their own individuality; it is the sum total of persons within a society which pursues the common good, which truly has a place for everyone (EG, 236)

This is what Pope Francis believes the Church can and must be—a community where there is a place for everyone. There is a place for the divorced and remarried as well as for the Lefebvrists. Those who are shocked by this are, whether they even know or admit it, scandalized by mysterious depths of the Gospel itself.

> The good news is the joy of the Father who desires that none of his little ones be lost, the joy of the Good Shepherd who finds the lost sheep and brings it back to the flock . . . The Gospel has an intrinsic principle of totality: it will always remain good news until it has been proclaimed to all people, until it has healed and strengthened every aspect of humanity, until it has brought all men and women together at table in God's kingdom (EG, 237)

As the pope says, there is a place for everyone in God's kingdom. And in just a few short years he's begun convincing people who were once far off that there is also a place for them in the Church. It is up to the Holy People of God, their pastors and their ministers to make that reality. Because, leaving aside all the various and important aspects of ecclesial reform, this is at the heart of Francis vision for the Church —there is a place for everyone.

Divorce and Remarriage

Geoffrey Robinson

Divorce

The practice of divorce in Israel when Jesus lived there was very different from the process of divorce with which we are familiar today. So, it would be a serious mistake to think of divorce as practised in Western society today and imagine that this is what the gospels are referring to whenever the word 'divorce' is used. There were two major points of difference.

The first is that the husband alone had the right to divorce. The wife had no appeal and, indeed, few rights of any kind in the matter. The only way in which she could secure a divorce was by putting pressure on her husband to divorce her.

The second is that there were no civil courts decreeing divorce, and no legally binding provisions for custody or maintenance. Indeed, there were no obligatory public procedures at all, and the matter was ruled by custom passed down within the tribe, clan or family. The most common requirement was the handing over to the wife by the husband of a certificate of divorce in the presence of two witnesses.

The grounds of divorce were very broad. From very early times ancient Israel was an honour-shame society, that is, one in which the honour of the male in the eyes of the community was of the utmost importance, and anything that was seen as bringing shame on him was treated with great seriousness. So if a man believed that his wife had brought shame on him by some extramarital sexual action, divorce was seen as obligatory - the only means of restoring his honour.[1] By

---

1. In the story told in the Gospel of Matthew, Joseph would have stood out from the crowd when, 'being a righteous man and unwilling to expose her to public

45

the time of Jesus there were very few restrictions on the husband's power to divorce.

Countless commentators have at this point referred to the controversy over the grounds of divorce between the scribal schools of Shammai and Hillell, but John P Meier insists that this controversy belongs to a later time. He quotes many sources to show that at the time of Jesus, divorce was an accepted fact of life in Jewish society and the grounds were very broad.[2]

It followed that the position of women in relation to marriage was precarious. And a woman divorced by her husband had no standing in the community and could easily find herself destitute.

We must see the statements of Jesus concerning divorce primarily in relation to this world of first century Israel. Only then can we apply them to our own time.

Adultery

The general understanding of adultery in our own times is that it is voluntary sexual intercourse between a married person and someone other than their spouse. Before we decide, however, that this is the meaning we must give to the term in the gospels, we need to consider two facts.

In the whole of the ancient world, not just in Israel, the basic unit of society was not the individual, but the family, so that a society was primarily seen as a collection of families. In each family the husband was lord and master. His wife or wives were quite literally his property, and adultery was then the violation of this *property right*. If a married woman had intercourse with any man other than her husband, it was always adultery, for it violated the property rights of her husband. If a man had intercourse with a married woman, it was also adultery, for he had violated the property rights of the woman's husband. But if a married man had intercourse with a single woman, it was not adultery, for the property rights of no husband were violated. Thus the term 'adultery' had little to do with the breaking of a promise or

---

disgrace, (he) planned to dismiss her quietly' (1:19). For other men the public disgrace of the unfaithful wife would have been seen as an essential part of the restoration of their own good name.

2. See *A Marginal Jew* (New Haven: Yale University Press, 2009), volume iv, 74–181.

with harm to a love relationship, but rather related to the stealing of the 'property' of a male.

The second fact is that in Matthew 5:25–28 Jesus is reported as saying, 'You have heard that it was said, "You shall not commit adultery". But I say to you that everyone who looks at a woman with lust has already committed adultery with her in his heart.' (5:27–28)

For Jesus sin existed in the mind and heart, and the external action was simply the result of the sin that had already occurred in the mind and heart. Thus, when divorce was contemplated, Jesus saw the adultery as occurring long before the formal divorce and remarriage, and long before any act of sexual intercourse had occurred. Adultery had occurred as soon as a man said to himself, 'I know this woman is married, but I want her and I'm going to do all I can to have her'.

There are five passages from the Second Testament that we must consider, and they may be divided into two pairs and one single text. Matthew 19:1–12 appears to be Matthew's reworking of Mark 10:2–12, so these two texts may be considered together. Matthew 5:31–32 and Luke16:18 both appear to depend on the same Q source, so they may also be considered together. That leaves the single text, Paul's statement in 1 Corinthians 7:10–15. I shall consider the texts in this order.

The Gospel of Mark

10.2. 'Some Pharisees came, and to test him they asked, "Is it lawful for a man to divorce his wife?"' The scene is presented as one of confrontation ('to test him'), with the Pharisees seeking ammunition to use against Jesus. For this reason, each of the four verses 3–6 begins with the word 'but', implying a continuing argument between the two sides. The question concerned an issue (the very fact of divorce) where the Pharisees thought they were on certain ground, for I have already noted that in ancient Israel divorce was simply a fact of life, not really queried by anyone. The basic First Testament text on divorce is to be found in Deuteronomy 24:1–4. It simply accepted divorce as a fact of life and added two requirements: the husband had to write out a bill of divorce and give it to his wife before two witnesses, and he could never marry her again once she had married another man. It says much that this text, dealing with the rare case of a man wishing to remarry his first wife after he had divorced her and she had been married to another man, became the standard text on divorce in the First Testament. It was the standard text because there was so little else on the subject. Divorce was a given, a fact of life.

3. (*But*) He answered them, 'What did Moses command you?' Instead of giving his own view, Jesus followed the constant scribal practice of answering a question with a question, taking the Pharisees back to the basis of their own beliefs in the law of Moses. His choice of the word 'command' was a tactical move, for the direct answer to this question would be that all that Moses had commanded was that, if a man divorced, he must give a written bill of divorce and may never marry the same woman again.

4. (*But*) They said, 'Moses allowed a man to write a certificate of dismissal and to divorce her.' Instead of saying what Moses *commanded*, the Pharisees spoke of what he had *allowed* and, in doing so, they were tacitly admitting that Moses had not commanded divorce. If divorce occurred, it was the people's, or at least the men's, own choice.

5. But Jesus said to them, 'Because of your hardness of heart he wrote this commandment for you.' In the First Testament the term 'hardheartedness' refers to the insensitivity that comes from continual disobedience to God.[3] The force of the verse is that the people had for so long been disobedient that they had lost their sensitivity to God, so that Moses had been able to do no more than salvage what he could by imposing some minimal restrictions.

6. 'But from the beginning of creation'. The Pharisees had asked, 'Is it lawful', and by this they meant 'Is it according to the law that came from God through Moses?' In his answer Jesus took the radical step of reinterpreting this law by asking, 'Is the law of Moses on this

---

3. The Greek word *sklerokardia* is still used in modern medicine. 'When Jesus affirmed that Moses framed the provision concerning the letter of dismissal out of regard to the people's hardness of heart, he was using an established legal category of actions allowed out of consideration for wickedness or weakness. What is involved is the lesser of two evils . . .' William L Lane, *The New International Commentary on the New Testament, The Gospel of Mark* (Grand Rapids: Erdmans, 1974), 355. '. . . hardness of heart is a major biblical theme. Since in biblical anthropology the heart is the source of understanding and judgment as well as emotions, hardness of heart involves closing off one's mind and emotions from the truth.' John R Donoghue and Daniel J Harrington, *The Gospel of Mark*, Sacra Pagina Series (Collegeville: Liturgical Press, 2002), 293.

point a true and full reflection of the mind of God?', and it was this question, not theirs, that he would now answer.[4] It is crucial to note that the entire argument of Jesus in this passage in Mark's Gospel is based on his appeal from a situation created by human insensitivity to the original intention of God.

'God made them male and female'. These words are a quotation from Genesis 1:27, stating that from the original intention of God human beings are essentially both male and female, with all their natural attraction and complementarity. The full quotation is:

> So God created humankind in his image,
> in the image of God he created them;
> male and female he created them.
> God blessed them, and God said to them,
> 'Be fruitful and multiply,
> and fill the earth and subdue it.

That human beings were both male and female was part of the creation, and the charge by God was given to them jointly and equally. There is no hint that it was really the male who was to "fill the earth and subdue it", while the female was to do nothing more than give birth to the babies and walk along meekly after him.

7. 'For this reason a man shall leave his father and mother and be joined to his wife, and the two shall become one flesh.' This verse also contains a quotation from Genesis, but this time from the earlier account of creation in the second chapter of Genesis (2:24), the story of Adam and Eve. The story begins with the words, 'God formed man from the dust of the ground, and breathed into his nostrils the breath of life; and the man became a living being' (2:7). This gave great dignity to the man in relation to other forms of life on earth, and yet it left the man in a state of restlessness and dissatisfaction because, though he had the divine breath in him, he was also made from 'the dust of the ground' and so could not be fully united to God.

---

4. 'The error of the Pharisees lay in their losing sight of this distinction (between an absolute divine command and a divine provision to deal with situations brought about by men's "hardness of heart") and so imagining that Deut 24:1 meant that God allowed divorce, in the sense that it had his approval and did not come under his judgment.' Augustine Stock OSB, *The Method and Message of Mark* (Wilmington: Michael Glazier, 1989), 265.

In order to assist him in this situation God said, 'It is not good that the man should be alone; I will make him a helper as his partner' (v 18), and the word used for 'helper', *ezer*, does not imply a subservient helper, for in the First Testament it is used also of God as our mighty helper. All the animals were brought to the man and he gave each one its name (2:19–20), implying, in Jewish understanding, that he both understood their nature and had power over them. Precisely for these reasons, however, the animals did not satisfy him—'but for the man there was not found a helper as his partner' (2:20b). So God formed a woman and brought her to him, and this time he could not give her a new name, but only his own name (*ish*) with a feminine ending (*ishshah*). He could not understand her depths as he did the animals, for she had the same divine breath in her as he did; and he had no power over her, for with that divine breath she was his equal. The words 'For this reason . . .' follow immediately, implying that the man did find true satisfaction in the woman and that this happened precisely because, sharing the same divine breath, she was his equal.[5] In the mind of Jesus, this was the original divine plan of marriage, and it was only in the security of this plan that marriage could fulfil its role in overcoming the restlessness of the human condition (Gen 2:18) and bringing a lasting happiness to people.

As Jesus grew up, he saw all around him a system of marriage that did not reflect this divine plan, and for two major reasons. First, it was based on a relationship of dominance-subservience, and for this very reason it created across the whole of society a form of marriage that would not and could not fulfil the deeper needs for which marriage had been created by God 'in the beginning'. Marriage can be either a relationship of power and authority between unequal partners or a love relationship between equal partners, but it cannot be both, and it cannot move backwards and forwards between the two at different times. The rights acquired in a wedding ceremony are either rights to property and ownership by the husband, or they are mutual rights to such things as justice, caring, respect and love, but they cannot

---

5.   I have taken this interpretation from Wilfrid J Harrington OP, *The Promise to Love* (London: Geoffrey Chapman, 1968). Harrington notes that the *ish-ishah* etymology is popular only, not exact. He calls it a typical Hebrew word play. He suggests that it is what the writer intended and helps to make sense of the passage.

be both. If they are rights to property, then the marriage contract is really between the father of the bride and the husband. It is a contract in which the father gives his property rights over his daughter to her husband, and she is simply the property or object that is passed over. It is only in a love relationship that the woman has something to give to her husband, so it is only in this case that the marriage is a true contract between the two of them. Furthermore, even if love is the basis on which a couple first enter a marriage, the fact that in Jewish law the man had dominance over the woman and could resort to power at any time placed severe strains on the love relationship. In Jewish law the authority of the husband was always there, and the wife's position was very weak.

The second reason follows from the first. One can always dispose of property, so if a man thinks of his wife as mere property, then she is easily disposable. Where there is gross inequality, divorce will always flourish. The questions of equality, marriage and divorce could not be separated, so in answer to a question concerning divorce, Jesus responded by first insisting that the original plan of God had been based on equality.

We know that Jesus recognised rights in women that the society around him did not and there are many scenes in which he showed a profound respect for their dignity. The power of men over divorce, the idea of a wife as property, the weak position of women in relation to marriage and the destitution of many divorced women constituted a *system* that Jesus found abhorrent, for it was contrary to his deep concern for justice and love. In responding to a question concerning divorce Jesus saw the need to attack this system and reform the entire understanding of marriage on a basis of equality. Without this reform of the entire system, it would never be possible to give an adequate answer to the question of divorce.

8. '. . .so that they are no longer two but one flesh.' These words have their mystery, but would seem to include a number of elements: the unity of flesh in sexual intercourse, the couple becoming as one before both the law and the community, their mutual love and common journey towards God, the two becoming one in their child, and the idea that marriage is such that part of the very being of each married person is the relationship to the other, so that to exclude this relationship is to deny part of one's own being.

9. 'Therefore what God has joined together, let no one separate.' The first meaning of these words is that they are a strong rejection of the universal idea of the times that men were the lords of marriage and freely decided its terms. They are a statement that for Jesus the true lord of marriage is God, for in such matters husband as well as wife must first obey God's will and seek to respect God's original intentions in establishing marriage.[6]

I suggest that there are two possible interpretations of these words. The first is the interpretation given by the Catholic Church at the Council of Trent and held to be infallibly binding for all time. In this interpretation what 'God has joined together' and human beings may not separate is each individual marriage. The words of Jesus would then imply that, in every single marriage ceremony, God joins the couple together in a divine bond that neither partner can ever break.[7]

The problem with this conclusion is that it does not follow from the argument that has gone before it, for that argument had not concerned divorce, but the divine plan for satisfaction and fulfilment through a relationship of equality and complementarity. The word 'therefore' in v 9 would be meaningless. Indeed, if this is a law concerning a divine bond, then the entire argument just given by Jesus is irrelevant, and one would have to query why that argument is there at all, for it neither explains nor adds anything to the statement concerning a divine law. Having just given women a whole new status in marriage,

---

6. 'The Mosaic provision in Deut 24:1–4 was in reality a witness to the gross evil which arose from, or even consisted in, a disregard of the creation ordinance of marriage as set forth in Gen 1:27; 2.24.' William L Lane, *The New International Commentary on the New Testament*, 355.

7. '5. If anyone says that the marriage bond can be dissolved because of heresy, or irksome cohabitation, or because of the wilful desertion of one of the spouses, anathema sit . . . 7. If anyone says that the church is in error for having taught and for still teaching that in accordance with the evangelical and apostolic doctrine (cf Mk10:1; 1Cor 7), the marriage bond cannot be dissolved because of adultery on the part of one of the spouses, and that neither of the two, not even the innocent one who has given no cause for infidelity, can contract another marriage during the lifetime of the other; and that the husband who dismisses an adulterous wife and marries again and the wife who dismisses an adulterous husband and marries again are both guilty of adultery, anathema sit.' Quoted from *The Christian Faith in the Doctrinal Documents of the Catholic Church*, edited by J Neuner and J Dupuis (London: Collins Liturgical Publications, London, 1983), 529.

Jesus would be leaving the abandoned wife in her predicament and doing nothing to help her. He would be doing nothing to redress the serious inequities that were present in marriage as it was practised in the society around him. He would not even be doing anything to curb divorce, for as long as marriage was unequal, divorce would flourish. He would, out of nowhere, be suddenly introducing a divine law that has no parallels to it anywhere in the gospels. While it has massive ecclesial authority behind it, there are serious problems with this interpretation.

The second interpretation is based on taking literally the word 'therefore' in v 9, that is, by insisting that the words 'What God has joined together let no human being separate' are a logical conclusion from what has been said in the argument just given. May I suggest that, if we take the word 'therefore' seriously, what God, in the mind of Jesus, had joined together 'in the beginning' was the two ideas of marriage and equality, while all around him Jesus saw that human beings had separated the two, substituting instead the two ideas of marriage and inequality. In terms of the bible story, putting together marriage and equality was the sole force that would take away the man's loneliness and give him a true partner. This is what God had joined together and no human beings were ever to separate. In the mind of God, marriage and equality were meant to be quite inseparable. At this point the entire passage becomes one coherent whole, with a logical argument and a logical conclusion.

For two thousand years people have understood the words 'Therefore what God has joined together, let no one separate' to refer to each individual marriage, and the Council of Trent gave most powerful backing to this idea. However, the words do not actually speak of each marriage; this is a conclusion that human beings have drawn. May I dare to suggest that this understanding needs to be looked at again.

Several times in the Gospel of Mark Jesus changed a question he was asked and then insisted on answering the changed question rather than the original one. This is exactly what he had done in v 6 of this same scene, as I noted above. The reason he did this is that, if we ask the wrong question, we will never find the right answer. In this case the original question was a wrong question because it assumed that men alone could divorce and that women were mere property. Jesus would not agree with these assumptions and so insisted on changing the question. In its essence, they had asked, 'What is divorce?', while Jesus insisted that the real question was 'What is marriage?' It was this question that he then sought to answer, and he gave no direct answer to the question concerning divorce, leaving his hearers to draw their own conclusions from what he had said about marriage.

I suggest, therefore, that what Jesus was speaking about here was what God had 'from the beginning of creation' intended marriage to be, and some of the powerful and compelling moral consequences that flow from this. For Jesus marriage is in the mind of God based on equality and, precisely for this reason, it is essentially permanent. The equality comes from God's creation, the permanence comes from the solemn and binding commitment that equal partners make to the marriage in accordance with God's plan for their fulfilment and happiness. There is even a form of indissolubility in marriage, in the sense that, without powerful reasons, neither partner is free to leave the marriage without being untrue to themselves.

10. 'Then in the house the disciples asked (*were asking*) him again about this matter.' The questions of the disciples were not polemic, but came from a genuine desire to understand, so in his reply Jesus did not seek to confront them as he had the Pharisees. At the same time, the imperfect tense of 'were asking' implies that the disciples were slow to accept the answer given them by Jesus and kept asking their questions.

11. 'He said to them, 'Whoever divorces his wife and marries another commits adultery against her'. The last two words ('against her') are of great importance, for by his use of these words Jesus was proclaiming that the violation of the rights of a wife was equally adultery. This was a logical conclusion from the argument he has just given concerning equality, but it was also a truly revolutionary idea, for it meant that for Jesus a wife had such rights and was, therefore, not the mere 'property' of her husband. This overturned the entire basis on which the family, and hence the whole of society, had been built. In its social impact it is arguably the most revolutionary statement in the whole of the gospels, for it demanded a completely new ordering of the entire society. It is small wonder that the disciples were slow to grasp the vast implications of what Jesus was saying. It is unspeakably sad that even two thousand years later the followers of Jesus have

still not caught up with his radicalism on the matter of the equality of male and female. The sheer amount of domestic violence in our societies is perhaps the clearest sign of this failure to grasp what Jesus was trying to say.

In the conversation with the disciples, I suggest that they brought up obvious points such as, 'Yes, all these beautiful things you are saying about equality and fulfilment are good and nice, but what about the hard reality of when a marriage is bringing only pain and dissatisfaction'. The response of Jesus was to take his argument further. We might summarise his earlier argument in vv 6–9 in this way, 'You will have a far happier and more fulfilling relationship if you in all things treat your wife as your equal, and commit yourself fully to the relationship'. In v 11 the argument goes further and is based on strict justice: 'It is not just a matter of your happiness. Your wife is truly your equal and has the same rights as you do. If you start looking outside your marriage, you will be committing adultery against her.'

Unlike legal consequences, however, moral consequences must always be estimated within the total context of all the circumstances of each marriage. There will, therefore, be circumstances which allow of a new marriage, for there will be circumstances that do not involve any form or degree of adultery. I shall return to this point.

12. 'And if she divorces her husband and marries another, she commits adultery'. It was Roman law that first gave to a wife the right to repudiate her husband, and commentators see this verse as a conclusion drawn by the Christian community from the words of Jesus rather than as a saying that came directly from Jesus himself[8].

Conclusions from the Text of Mark

I believe that in this passage Jesus was concerned to do far more than make some changes to divorce practice. He wanted to do away with the entire *system* of both marriage and divorce then in practice and with the attitudes that went behind the system. I believe that any interpretation that has him doing less than this fails to see the full force of the passage.

---

8. This verse in effect has the church saying to women under Roman law, 'Don't start getting legalistic and claiming that what Jesus said doesn't apply to you because, against his Jewish background, he spoke only of men. It applies to you too'.

Jesus was confronted with a situation where the males in the community were collectively the lords of marriage as a social institution and each man was then lord of his own marriage, with a broad power to divorce his wife. Women were mere property and had no say in the matter. Jesus rebelled against these attitudes, asserting that they came from 'hardness of heart' and that they had not been the original intention of God. He insisted that it is God who is the sole lord of marriage, so all people, male and female, must seek to be true to those things that are inherent in marriage as God created it.

He said that God in the beginning created human beings male and female, and created them in such a manner that their greatest happiness and growth, their best chance of learning to live creatively with the restlessness of the human condition, are to be found in committing themselves unreservedly and *as equals* to a lasting union in accordance with a divine plan, and in then doing everything in their power to make sure that the union in fact flourishes and lasts. Each of the couple, therefore, has a powerful *moral* obligation towards the other.

In other words, what Jesus could not agree with in this scene in Mark was a *system* that he saw as an *adulterous system*, understanding the word 'adulterous' in the sense I have already indicated. For men to consider themselves lords of their marriage and free to divorce and remarry as it suited them, without any consideration for their wife, was, in the mind of Jesus, to be already deeply immersed in an adulterous mindset. In accordance with everything we know about him as a *person*, Jesus strongly attacked this system and replaced it with both an insistence on unheard of rights in the woman and the profoundly challenging ideal of regaining the creation.

If marriage today is different from that of the society in which Jesus lived, the message of this passage is as relevant today as it was then, for examples of inequality in the thinking of men are universal. In the Western world of today there is arguably a far greater equality in marriage than there was in the time of Jesus, and this is a good thing. But the fact that nearly half of all these marriages end in divorce argues strongly that all is far from well, and that we need to return to the ideals of Jesus again and again.

Matthew 19:1–12

> Some Pharisees came to him, and to test him they asked, 'Is it lawful for a man to divorce his wife for any cause?' He answered, 'Have you not read that the one who made them at the beginning made them male and female, and said, 'For this reason a man shall leave his father and mother and be joined to his wife, and the two shall become one flesh'? So they are no longer two, but one flesh. Therefore what God has joined together, let no one separate.' They said to him, 'Why then did Moses command us to give a certificate of dismissal and to divorce her?' He said to them, 'It was because you were so hard-hearted that Moses allowed you to divorce your wives, but from the beginning it was not so. And I say to you, whoever divorces his wife, except for unchastity, and marries another, commits adultery.' (19:1–10)

Though there are differences,[9] there are also obvious similarities between this scene and the one in Mark we have already considered. Indeed, this scene is usually accepted as little more than Matthew's reworking of Mark's scene according to his own criteria. In Mark the question had concerned the lawfulness of divorce as such, while in Matthew the question appears to assume the lawfulness of divorce and raises a question concerning the grounds ('for any cause').

In calling back immediately to the intention of God in the creation, Matthew presents Jesus as claiming the moral high ground from the beginning of the discussion and forcing his opponents to prove their case. They introduce the law of Moses, but they go further than is lawful, for they use the word 'command' to cover both the written document of dismissal and the very right to divorce, and we have already seen that, while Moses commanded the written document of dismissal, he did not command divorce. Jesus corrects them in his second answer, saying that Moses allowed, not commanded, divorce, and did so only because of their hardheartedness. For a second time he calls back to 'the beginning', that is, the original intention of God in the creation. His conclusion is the same as in Mark, 'Whoever

---

9. 'Matthew has . . . restructured the argument so that the positive argument about God's will for men and women from the creation comes first and the concession made by Moses comes second.' Harrington, *The Promise to Love*, 274–275.

divorces his wife and marries another, commits adultery'. Though the words 'against her' are not stated explicitly, they are implicit, for adultery has to be committed against someone, and it is clearly the wife who is intended. Once again, the statement that a man could commit adultery against his wife was startling, radical and revolutionary in its implications.

The conclusions that I drew from the Gospel of Mark can be drawn from this passage in Matthew also, for it contains the same essential argument: a call back from the current *system* of marriage and divorce to God's original intention in creating marriage, the same two quotations concerning the equality and complementarity of man and woman, and a conclusion that the man could commit adultery, as Jesus understood the term, against his wife. Equally with Mark, it is the condemnation of a *system* of marriage and divorce that all too easily involved an adulterous mindset and harmed the very purposes for which marriage had been created 'in the beginning'.

Except for Unchastity

In this passage we must also consider the extra phrase introduced both here and in the passage in Matthew that I shall consider next: 'except in the case of *porneia*'. The word *porneia* can cover any form of sexual impropriety, and is better translated by the broad word 'unchastity'.

In understanding this phrase I believe that it is important that we not see Jesus as doing no more than agree with those (a fairly small minority) who believed that divorce was permitted only in the case of adultery by the wife, for then his taking the high ground by twice calling back to the will of God in the creation would be meaningless. His reply would no longer be radical or revolutionary,[10] and it would still include the idea that only men could initiate divorce and that women had no rights in the matter. In other words, Jesus would still be approving the *system* of marriage and divorce then in practice.

---

10. 'The addition (of the exceptive clause) not only softens the ethics of the kingdom, but it also stands in tension with the absolutism of v 6, weakens the argument of vv 7–8, and makes the disciples' comments in v 10 and Jesus' statements in vv 11–12 less appropriate than would be the case of an absolute prohibition of divorce.' Hagner, *The Promise to Love*, volume 2, 549.

It seems to me that the very essence of this scene is that Jesus was asked to decide between two schools of thought and gave an answer that was more radical than either. I believe that we are on far firmer ground if we see Matthew as being fully as radical as Mark, and this essentially demanded a rejection of the entire *system* of marriage and divorce then in practice.

> That Jesus was demanding a fidelity to marriage and a commitment to pledged love that went beyond the expectations of his contemporaries of whatever school of thought is obvious from the reaction of his disciples.[11]

The male disciples (10–12) correctly saw in the words of Jesus the taking away of traditional male rights in this matter:

> His disciples said to him, 'If such is the case of a man with his wife, it is better not to marry.' But he said to them, 'Not everyone can accept this teaching, but only those to whom it is given. For there are eunuchs who have been so since birth, and there are eunuchs who have been made eunuchs by others, and there are eunuchs who have made themselves eunuchs for the sake of the kingdom of heaven. Let anyone accept this who can.'[12]

There is an immense literature on the meaning of the exceptive clauses, and most explanations can be reduced to two. Common to both is that the words do not come from Jesus himself, but were added by the early church.

> If the Matthean exceptive clause had been a part of the original form of the prohibition, it is extremely difficult to understand how and why Paul, Mark and Luke would all have come up with absolute forms of the prohibition.[13]

---

11. Michael Fallon MSC, *The Gospel According to Saint Matthew* (Sydney: Chevalier Press, 1997), 261.
12. 'The disciples speak as if the attraction of marriage depended on easy divorce.' Harrington, *The Promise to Love*, 274.
13. John P Meier, *A Marginal Jew*, volume iv, 104.

The first explanation is that the words are a true exception. One version (among many) of this is that it is possible that Jewish followers of Jesus might have accepted his ideal of returning to God's original intentions in creating marriage, and even accepted that women had rights, and (with great difficulty under the strong influence of the powerful personality of Jesus) that they even had equal dignity and rights. But, with a lifetime of a culture of honour-shame behind them, they simply could not bring themselves to accept that a man should remain with a wife guilty of adultery or some other serious sexual impropriety. That was altogether too much and the weight of their cultural heritage was too powerful. In this interpretation the early church, through Matthew, is allowing for this attitude.

This interpretation presupposes that Matthew realised that the words of Jesus had been a statement of powerful moral obligation, to which there can in serious circumstances be exceptions, rather than a divine law about an unbreakable bond, to which there can be no exceptions.

The other explanation of the exceptive clause is that it refers to a marriage within the forbidden degrees of kinship laid down in the First Testament. These laws went beyond those of most other nations, so it was always possible that Christian converts from paganism might already be in a marriage that was forbidden by Jewish law, and hence that would scandalise Jewish converts. The Jews considered such a marriage to be a *porneia*, an unchastity, and believed that in these circumstances divorce was not divorce at all, but the putting aside of a wife whom one should not have married in the first place. The exceptive clause would then have been an addition by the early church to cover situations that had arisen and were causing scandal to Jewish converts. Chapter 15 of the Acts of the Apostles tells the story of the First Council of Jerusalem, when the early church introduced laws precisely in order to avoid scandal to Jewish converts. There are, however, some serious problems with this interpretation,[14] and I personally favour the first explanation.

---

14. 1) The context does not indicate at all that Matthew wants to take *porneia* in such a narrow sense and to refer his exception only to the former Gentiles. 2) Correspondingly, no single Church father and no single interpreter up until the modern time would have understood what he was truly concerned about. 3) In Leviticus 18 the word *porneia* is missing. 4) *Parektos logou porneias* is a clear reference to Dt 24:1, 'but then it must deal with the reasons for the divorce

I am unable to take the matter further in terms of analysis of the texts. In accordance with the overriding idea of this article, therefore, I turn to the *person* of Jesus and all we know about his values and how he acted. When the texts are seen in this light, I repeat that I believe it is important that we not adopt an interpretation that would have Jesus doing no more than agree with one school of thought, while leaving the *system* of marriage and divorce in place. I suggest that our minimum conclusion must be to assume that there is no contradiction between this scene, the earlier scene in this same Gospel that I shall consider next, and the scene in Mark. I suggest that we must see Matthew as being as radical as Mark and, like Mark, both speaking the language of moral obligation rather than of law and rejecting the entire current *system* of marriage and divorce.

Matthew 5:31–32

We now come to the second pair of texts, both seeming to derive from the same statement in the common Q source.

> It was also said, 'Whoever divorces his wife, let him give her a certificate of divorce.' But I say to you that anyone who divorces his wife, except on the ground of unchastity, causes her to commit adultery; and whoever marries a divorced woman commits adultery (5:31–32).

I have already considered the meaning of the words 'except on the ground of unchastity' and shall make no further comment here.

The context of the saying being considered here is that of the Sermon on the Mount (5:1–7:29) and, in particular, the section contained in 5:17-48. It begins by saying,

> Do not think that I have come to abolish the law or the prophets; I have not come to abolish but to fulfil.[15]

---

of legitimate and not with the invalidity of illegitimate marriages'. Ulrich Luz, *Matthew 1–7, A Commentary* (Minneapolis: Augsburg Fortress, 1989), 304–305.

15. 'The ethical teaching of Jesus that follows in this sermon . . . has such a radical character and goes so much against what was the commonly accepted understanding of the commands of the Torah that it is necessary at the outset to vindicate Jesus' full and unswerving loyalty to the law.' Donald A Hagner,

Over the following twenty-eight verses (21–48) Jesus then spells out what he means by 'not abolish but fulfil'[16] in a series of sayings in the form, 'You have heard that it was said . . ., but I say to you . . .'.

> You have heard that it was said to those of ancient times, 'You shall not murder'. . . But I say to you that if you are angry with a brother or sister . . . (21–26) . . . 'You shall not commit adultery'. But I say to you that everyone who looks at a woman with lust . . . (27–30) . . . It was said, 'whoever divorces his wife . . . but I say to you . . . (31–32) . . . 'you shall not swear falsely' . . . But I say to you, Do not swear at all . . . (33–37) . . . 'An eye for an eye and a tooth for a tooth.' But I say to you . . . if anyone strikes you on the right cheek, turn the other also . . . (38–42) . . . 'You shall love your neighbour and hate your enemy.' But I say to you, Love your enemies (43–47) . . . Be perfect, therefore, as your heavenly Father is perfect. (48)

Though most commentators call these sayings 'antitheses', the word

> fits the rhetorical pattern but not the content. In some cases Jesus expresses agreement with the biblical teaching but urges his followers to go deeper or to the root of the commandment (murder>anger, adultery>lust, retaliation>non-resistance). In other cases Jesus' teaching can seem to go so far as to make the biblical commandment useless (divorce, oaths, love of neighbour.)[17]

Matthew 1–13, Word Biblical Commentary (Dallas: Word Books Publishers, 1993), 103. 'These were the words of a strict Jewish Christian community seeking to maintain absolute obedience to the letter of the Law, probably in opposition to a more liberal interpretation such as those represented by Stephen' (cf Acts 7:48ff, 8:1) and later by Paul (Gal 2:2–6, 11:6; Acts 15). Edward Schweizer, *The Gospel According to Matthew* (London: SPCF, 1975), 104.

16. 'When considered in itself, the opposition of 5:17 allows us to say that "to fulfil" is contrasted with 'to abolish', that is, to dismantle, tear down, and thus make invalid, annul . . . Fulfilling means, therefore, having a constructive attitude towards Scripture and considering it important, not null.' Daniel Patte, *The Gospel According to Matthew* (Philadelphia: Fortress Press, 1987), 72.

17. Daniel J Harrington SJ, *The Gospel of Matthew*, Sacra Pagina Series (Collegeville: The Liturgical Press, 1991), 90.

Furthermore, the sayings concern different orders of law from the Torah: while the first two concern the Ten Commandments, the others do not and, indeed, there was no law forbidding divorce itself.

The first thing that appears to be clear is that, while Jesus is quoting laws from the First Testament, he is not simply replacing them with new laws. He is leaving the laws in place ('not abolish') and then expressing moral principles that show the more perfect way to observe the value that is behind the law ('but fulfil'). To be perfect as the heavenly father is perfect or to turn the other cheek are not new laws. We are not morally deficient if we fail to be as perfect as the heavenly Father and we are not breaking a law if we swear an oath in court or fail to turn the other cheek and allow someone to strike us a second time.

> Interpreters of these verses must be careful not to translate into legal statute what is presented as an evangelic counsel. That is, it ought not to be treated differently than the other antitheses, none of which has been or can be converted into law.[18]

The new sayings of Jesus go beyond the external action demanded by the law to moral principles concerning the internal attitudes that lead to the breaking of the law.[19] In this they may be called prescriptive ideals, that is, they are ideals, not laws, but they are prescriptive, for we are meant, and indeed obliged, to strive after them. I do not commit sin if I fail to have warm feelings for my enemies, but I do fail as a follower of Jesus if I do not even see loving my enemies as an ideal that calls to me with genuine power and urgency. I do not fail morally if I am not as perfect as the heavenly Father, but I do fail as a Christian if I do not see being as perfect as the heavenly Father as a goal that might guide my life.

Furthermore, the language of this section needs to be taken into account, for it is Semitic language and so is concrete rather than abstract and involves what our modern Western minds would

---

18. Douglas RA Hare, *Matthew* (Louisville: John Knox Press, 1993), 54
19. 'Common to most is the sense that righteous behaviour has to do with the heart and with attitude rather than with mere conformity with external prescription.' Brendan Byrne, *Lifting the Burden, Reading Matthew's Gospel in the Church Today* (Sydney: St Paul's Publications, 2004), 58.

consider serious exaggeration or overstatement, even extravagance. It is a language that appears to be typical of the *person* of Jesus, for example:

> If any of you put a stumbling block before one of these little ones who believe in me, it would be better for you if a great millstone were hung around your neck and you were thrown into the sea (Mk 9:42).
>
> It is easier for a camel to go through the eye of a needle than for someone who is rich to enter the kingdom of God (Mk 10:25).
>
> Why do you see the speck in your neighbour's eye, but do not notice the log in your own eye? (Mt 7:3).
>
> So therefore, none of you can become my disciple if you do not give up all your possessions (Lk 14:33).
>
> It is easier for heaven and earth to pass away, than for one stroke of a letter in the law to be dropped (Lk 16:17).
>
> Whoever comes to me and does not hate father and mother, wife and children, brothers and sisters, yes, and even life itself, cannot be my disciple (Lk 14:26).

It is obvious that these sayings cannot be taken in a slavishly literal manner.

This type of language abounds in the context of the series of prescriptive ideals that surround this saying on divorce. There we are told by Jesus not to be angry, though in fact we have no direct control over our feelings and cannot prevent feelings of anger whenever a serious wrong is done to us. We are told that if we say to someone, 'You fool', we 'will be liable to the hell of fire', though no one would take this literally. We are told not to look at a woman with lust, though the very continuance of the human race demands that there be sexual desire. We are told that, if our eye causes us to sin, we should tear it out and throw it away, and no church has ever suggested that we should take these words literally. We are told that we should never swear oaths, and yet both church and state routinely administer oaths. We are told to turn the other cheek, to give a cloak as well as a tunic and to walk a second mile, though no one interprets these as literal obligations. We are told to love our enemies, though once again we have no direct control over our feelings. Finally, we are told to be perfect as the heavenly Father is perfect, though this is manifestly impossible and we will never come even remotely close to living up to this ideal.

The saying on divorce comes in the middle of these prescriptive ideals (31–32) and this context cannot be ignored. It would surely be nonsense to say that the statements surrounding this one are all prescriptive ideals, not laws, but that the one on divorce is a strict law rather than a prescriptive ideal. It would be nonsense to say that all the surrounding statements use exaggerated Semitic language, but this one uses only literal language. It follows that the saying on divorce must also be seen as a prescriptive ideal rather than as a law. The message must surely be that people are not necessarily committing sin if they divorce, for there may be cases where it is justified, but they are failing if they do not see permanency as a powerful and binding ideal, something that they must strive for with all their might.

These considerations strongly reinforce the idea that the words contained in Mark 10 and Matthew 19 are forceful statements of moral obligation rather than statements of law.

Matthew goes further than Mark, for Mark had spoken only of the case where the man had divorced his wife and married another. Matthew takes two other cases. In the first he has Jesus saying that, if a man divorces his wife, he is causing the wife to commit adultery, presumably by marrying another man. In the second case, he imagines a man marrying a woman who has been divorced, and speaks of this as adultery on his part. Mark had placed the accent on the act of divorcing a wife, while Matthew looks to the remarriage after the divorce, not by the man who divorced his wife, but by the woman who is divorced and by the man marrying her.

The two statements in Matthew 5:32 sound harsher than those of Mark, for they might seem to include the woman divorced by her husband and left destitute, but we must keep firmly in mind the fact that in Matthew they are presented as prescriptive ideals. It follows that Jesus is not saying that either the wife or the second man is necessarily committing sin through a second marriage. What, then, is the prescriptive ideal he is pointing to? I shall return to these questions later.

The Gospel of Luke 16:18

> Anyone who divorces his wife and marries another commits
> adultery, and whoever marries a woman divorced from her
> husband commits adultery.

This saying is in language very similar to Matthew 5:31–32, so that
most scholars believe that both texts come from the Q document that
lies behind much of Matthew and Luke.

As it stands in the Gospel of Luke, the saying has its difficulties, for
the context does nothing to assist us. Beginning in chapter 15 we have
a series of parables (the lost sheep, the lost drachma, the prodigal son
and the dishonest steward), then we have four sayings that do not
appear to have any direct connection either to the parables or to each
other, and then we have another parable (the rich man and Lazarus).

The saying on divorce is the fourth of the sayings in the middle
of these parables. The first saying may be seen as connected to the
parable of the unjust steward immediately preceding it, for it speaks
of love of money. But the second deals with the kingdom taking the
place of the law and the prophets, and the third with the fact that
no detail of the law will be abolished.[20] The fourth then deals with
divorce.[21] So far as can be seen, the saying stands on its own without
any particular context.[22]

---

20. 'The second set of sayings in this Lucan editorial unit preceding the parable of
the rich man and Lazarus has almost nothing to do with material possessions or
ambitious esteem before other human beings, topics of Jesus' comments in vv
1–15.' Joseph A Fitzmyer, *The Gospel According to Luke* (New York: Anchor Bible,
Doubleday and Co 1985), volume 2, 1114.

21. 'The third saying in this editorial unit seems to move to an entirely different
topic—even less related to the general theme of ch.16 than the sayings on the
law in the two preceding verses—viz the prohibition of divorce (v 16).' Joseph A
Fitzmyer, *The Gospel According to Luke,*1119.

22. In the commentaries I have studied there are many attempts to give a unity to
these sayings, but no two seem to agree. Brendan Byrne expresses a common
opinion when he says, 'It is hard to account for the series of sayings lying between
the two parables in this chapter. The sayings seem disconnected, both with the
wider context and among each other.' *The Hospitality of God, A Reading of Luke's
Gospel* (Sydney: St Paul's Publications, 2002), 134. Furthermore, the middle two
sayings are not at all clear in themselves and there is much debate over their
meaning. Commentaries that are most helpful in understanding other parts of
Luke's Gospel seem to be at something of a loss here. See, for example, Luke
Timothy Johnson, *The Gospel of Luke*, Sacra Pagina Series (Collegeville: Liturgical

This lack of context creates problems for an interpreter. There is, however, no reason to think that the Gospel of Luke wishes to contradict the Gospels of Mark or Matthew. Good practice in biblical interpretation would rather say that we should interpret the brief statement without a context in Luke in the light of the longer statements with context given in both Mark and Matthew. We may conclude that Luke is also speaking the language of moral obligation in justice and love rather than law. To dismiss a wife because a man has met another woman he prefers and to leave his wife and the children of the marriage without a man in a world that was built on families was a violation of both justice and love and, therefore, in the eyes of Jesus, adultery. If to the words of Luke we add all the same author says about the *person* of Jesus, we must once again see Jesus insisting, with all the force at his command, on the rights and equal dignity of the woman and on the moral obligations that flowed from this.

In common with the first saying on divorce in Matthew (5:31–32), Luke also has Jesus speaking of the man who marries a divorced woman. Once again I shall leave comment on this point until after we have looked at the statement of Paul.

The First Letter to thee Corinthians 7:10–15

> To the married I give this command—not I but the Lord—that the wife should not separate from her husband, but if she does separate, let her remain unmarried or else be reconciled to her husband, and that the husband should not divorce his wife.
>
> To the rest I say—I and not the Lord—that if any believer has a wife who is an unbeliever and she consents to live with him, he should not divorce her. And if any woman has a husband who is an unbeliever, and he consents to live with her, she should not divorce him . . .
>
> But if the unbelieving partner separates, let it be so; in such a case the brother or sister is not bound. It is to peace that God has called you . . .

This letter of Paul to the Corinthians was written around the year 54–55 CE, some fifteen years before any of the gospels, so it is the first testimony to the teaching of Jesus on the subject of divorce.

Press, 1991), 250–251 and 254–255.

Paul introduces the topic by saying that he is answering some questions that the Christian community in the city of Corinth had referred to him ('Now concerning the matters about which you wrote.... 7:1).[23] What follows has been described as similar to listening to one end of a telephone conversation,[24] and Paul had no idea that his simple reply to a letter would one day be considered part of the New Testament and analysed in minute detail. We would love to know the exact questions he was asked, but there is considerable difficulty in determining this.[25]

This creates a problem when we come to the question of divorce. In vv 10 and 12 Paul appears to create an antithesis: 'To the married I give this command—not I but the Lord—. . . To the rest I say—I and not the Lord'. But who are 'the rest'? They are not 'the unmarried', for this would not make sense of the text. It is possible that 'the married' means those in a marriage of two Christians, while 'the rest' indicates Christians in a mixed marriage with a non-Christian, but this is far from certain.

It appears that the particular case referred to Paul concerns the situation of a Christian whose non-Christian spouse has left and sought a divorce. In his answer, it appears that Paul first quotes his understanding of what Jesus had said ('not I but the Lord'), and then gives his own application of this teaching to the particular case that the community had referred to him ('I and not the Lord').

In presenting his understanding of what Jesus had said, Paul is close to what the gospels will later say. He is unusual in speaking first of the wife leaving her husband, and this implies a practice of divorce different from that of the Jewish world in which Jesus had spoken. It reflects the fact that he was writing to Christians in the Greek city of Corinth who had been influenced by Greek and Roman practices of

---

23. 'The matters which they raised can be gathered in part from Paul's introducing them with "now concerning"; by this criterion they included: marriage and divorce (7:1), virginity (7:25), food offered to idols (8:1), spiritual gifts (12:1), the collection for Jerusalem (16:1), and Apollos (16:12)'. *1 and 2 Corinthians*, edited by FF Bruce, New Century Bible, (London: Oliphants, 1971), 66.

24. 'Paul was asked some definite questions, and he answered them; he was not concerned with developing a full theology of the subject.' Dennis Murphy msc, *The Apostle of Corinth* (Melbourne: Campion Press, 1966), 166.

25. It is most probable that he is quoting or at least summarising the first question when he says in 7:1, 'It is well for a man not to touch a woman.'

divorce. It is also possible, of course, that this was the particular case that had been referred to him.

In applying this teaching of Jesus to the case presented to him, there is no scriptural basis on which to claim that Paul understands himself to be quoting a law laid down by Jesus and then, by virtue of some claim of delegated divine authority, either changing that law or dispensing from it (the so-called 'Pauline Privilege'). It surely makes more sense to say that Paul is quoting the serious moral obligation, the prescriptive ideal, of which Jesus had spoken in relation to marriage and divorce ('not I but the Lord') and is then applying that moral obligation to a particular situation that had arisen in Corinth ('I and not the Lord'). In this application he says that a Christian should not initiate a divorce, but that if the non-Christian partner leaves the marriage, 'let it be so'.

In the circumstances presented Paul appears to acknowledge that the words of Jesus do not constitute a law or an absolute prohibition of divorce. This saying of Paul, therefore, supports the idea of moral obligations and prescriptive ideals rather than laws, for if Paul saw the words of Jesus as a universal law, it is impossible to understand how he could have claimed the authority to dispense from it. He refrains, however, from spelling out the details of his answer, for in saying, 'let it be so', he does not speak explicitly of remarriage. I suggest that he implies that on that subject his readers should listen to what Jesus had said about powerful prescriptive ideals.

Remarriage

Perhaps recent history shows us why Jesus stopped short of making a law, but did use such forceful and extravagant language in speaking of an ideal. For many centuries in the Christian world all divorce was forbidden, and this caused most serious hardship for large numbers of individuals. Then civil divorce was introduced, at first on very restricted grounds, but eventually, and inevitably, on virtually any ground. The attitudes created by this practice have in their turn affected the manner in which many people approach marriage and the expectations they bring to it, leading to further divorce. Through these attitudes, many people and, of course, many children, are badly hurt. The present situation, in which marriage itself seems to be in danger, can hardly be seen as an ideal by anyone.

I suggest that it is at this point that we can perhaps see why Jesus spoke, not only of the man who divorces his wife and marries another (Mk 10:11; Mt19:9; Lk 16:18), but also of the woman who is divorced and the man who marries her (Mk 10:12; Mt 5:32; Lk 16:18). We have seen in our own day that, when divorce thoroughly permeates the thinking of a community, and marriage is so little respected that very large numbers of people dispense with it entirely, one of the effects is that married persons are no longer seen as 'off limits'. If one is attracted to a married person, the fact of the marriage often seems to be of little concern in pursuing that attraction. In the thinking of Jesus, such a person has adulterous desires and gives adulterous effect to them, and the married person who responds has equally adulterous desires. Often the other partner is left with little choice other than to agree to the divorce.

At the time of Jesus, women in Israel could not divorce their husbands, but they could put pressure on their husbands to divorce them. If there was an invasion of the marriage by another man, the husband could be left with little choice other than to divorce. In the texts we have been considering, it is obvious that Jesus has gone well beyond the formal act of adultery and has spoken of persons as adulterous when their thinking was adulterous. I have already noted that v 5:32 of Matthew must be interpreted in the light of v 28, where 'looking at a woman with lust' is seen as adultery.

In this sense, the man who has invaded a marriage and the married woman who has responded to him are already adulterous before any act of intercourse has taken place, and certainly before any remarriage occurs. At all times it was not law or external actions that concerned Jesus, but the violation of a solemn commitment of love and the important rights that flowed from this in justice.

I suggest that it was this 'culture' of divorce in his own day that Jesus was seeking to confront. He would not forbid divorce altogether, for this would cause unbearable hardship for some, and in any case he had not come to make a whole series of laws on all subjects. But, with the divorce practice of his own time and place before his eyes, he would have nothing to do with the idea of divorce on any terms and without concern for the harm caused to others or to the institution of marriage itself. The culture of divorce around Jesus was powerful and he had to break through it at all costs and make people think. His response to this dilemma was to call people back to God's original intention in creating male and female and to speak the language of prescriptive ideals, powerful and binding moral obligations that his followers must treat with the utmost seriousness. He would never be content with paying lip service to the idea of permanency while in practice condoning a lax attitude, and so in forceful Semitic language he insisted on total seriousness by presenting the most radical ideal and challenge possible.

When Jesus said, 'If your right eye causes you to sin, tear it out and throw it away', he did not mean this to be taken literally. On the other hand, he certainly did not want anyone to think that it was mere exaggeration and could be ignored. By means of this forceful and concrete language he was saying, 'If something has become an obstacle between you and God, get rid of it. Do whatever you have to do, but get rid of it. Be radical. Treat the matter with the utmost seriousness and accept no compromise.' Instead of using more abstract statements like these, the Semitic Jesus used the more graphic and deliberately shocking pictorial language of tearing out an eye to express the same idea.

I suggest that when he said three verses later, 'Whoever marries a divorced woman commits adultery' he was again using graphic and even shocking pictorial language to express as forcefully as possible the idea that when a marriage is ignored in the pursuit of desire, there is a most serious danger of committing adultery in the heart. He was saying that a man who harboured such thoughts in his heart was in exactly the same position as a man who took a woman from her husband and began living openly with her.

He was insisting that marriage is to be taken with the utmost seriousness, that the words 'for better for worse . .' 'til death do us part' are to be said with all one's heart and soul and being. He was reminding us that we are shaped by the promises we make and the way we stand by them, for they enter into our being and make us the persons we are. He was stressing that, more than almost anything else in human life, the commitment given on a wedding day both expresses and shapes the very persons we are. He was aware of just how much of their happiness and well-being individuals place in the hands of another person on a wedding day, and was insisting that their partners accept this gift as a most sacred trust. He was pointing to the most serious danger of both individuals and whole communities stepping on to the slippery slope that leads to the breakdown of the very institution of marriage.

At the same time, he was acknowledging the seriousness of the difficulties that can arise in marriage. He was acknowledging that situations can occur where separation and divorce are the only intelligent and proper solution. He did his best to combine these two sides to the argument by means of a prescriptive ideal and a commanding, even shocking challenge.

The Ideal

Once we begin to speak the language of prescriptive ideal and commanding challenge rather than law, the vast variety of particular situations that can arise must be taken into account. The words of Jesus, as applied to a man who abandons an older wife and children solely in order to marry a younger one, cannot be applied without further thought to, for example, a woman with young children abandoned by a husband and left destitute.

What was the ideal, then, that Jesus was speaking of in his words about remarriage? Let me start with a case I have met in pastoral practice. A couple married, but six months later the wife was involved in a car accident that caused serious brain damage and left her unable to communicate or even recognise people. I met the couple some thirty years after this, and found that the man had not remarried but was still devoted to his wife and looking after her every day. He was not a Catholic, so Catholic teachings were not part of his thinking. But he loved his wife and had committed himself to her 'for better for worse, for richer for poorer, in sickness and in health, till death do us part'. I have no desire to make a law for all people out of this free decision of one person, but must we not admit that there was much that is admirable and even heroic in his fidelity? Had not this man in some manner regained the creation?

We may add the not uncommon statement of separated or even divorced persons that 'I couldn't go out with anyone else yet. I still feel married.' When a total commitment was given on a wedding day, many people do not find it easy to leave a marriage behind, no matter what has happened.

When people today talk about divorce, they usually start from the moment when a marriage has completely broken down and ask, 'How should we respond compassionately to this situation?' But Jesus wanted his followers to put this situation into a context. He wanted to ask them, 'How do you as a young person make sure you yourself are as fully prepared for marriage as your age allows? How should you choose a partner? How seriously do the two of you prepare for your wedding day? How totally do you commit yourselves to each other in that ceremony? How do you live your married life? How do you handle the difficulties that arise? How much are you affected by the culture of divorce around you and how do you respond to it? Do you truly share Christian ideals for marriage and how hard are you willing to work to achieve them? Have you really tried all other alternatives before you even look at separation and divorce?' Only in this light can the question of remarriage be seen in context. Only then is the ideal of Jesus still alive. The only people not profoundly hurt by the breakdown of a marriage are those who put little into it in the first place. Jesus was radical and those who genuinely seek to follow him need to be radical too.

In the light of these considerations, it would seem that for a follower of Jesus divorce could be accepted in only three cases:

- when a marriage partner has departed and will never return;
- when there is a genuine conflict between the obligations of married life and other more serious obligations, for example, basic obligations towards children or the duty to preserve one's own life and sanity;
- when, despite all efforts, including the seeking of assistance from others through counselling, the living of anything that could be called 'married life' has become an impossibility.

It is in interpreting these three criteria and applying them to a particular situation that the strength of the challenge of Jesus would have to be kept firmly in mind.

Is this combination of prescriptive ideal and radical and shocking challenge more in conformity with everything we know about the *person* of Jesus Christ than the idea of his using divine authority to decree a law? Is it in conformity with the story of his own life and death on a cross? On this basis can we reconcile the words of the gospels with all we know about the *person* who spoke them?

Conclusion

It is obvious that, even for those Christians who most earnestly seek the will of Jesus in this matter of divorce and remarriage, there are many problems in the evidence of the Second Testament, for uncertainties abound in every single one of the texts. Is this an indication that, while we must have the greatest respect for the Scriptures, God will not solve all our problems for us, and we cannot put all the responsibility onto God? Must we not rather take a large measure of both personal and collective responsibility in this delicate and difficult field?

I fear that some Protestant Churches have in practice been caught into ways of acting on this subject that do not do justice to the powerful call of Jesus. At the same time there must be queries as to whether the teaching of the Catholic Church, as set out in canons 5 and 7 of the Canons on the Sacrament of Matrimony of the Council of Trent,[26] truly respects the teaching and the *person* of Jesus as revealed to us in the Second Testament. I hope that I have shown that these canons of Trent are selective in the parts of the Second Testament they quote and fall well short of reflecting the entirety of the evidence. Surely there are matters here that are in urgent need of serious discussion.

---

26. '5. If anyone says that the marriage bond can be dissolved because of heresy, or irksome cohabitation, or because of the wilful desertion of one of the spouses, anathema sit . . . 7. If anyone says that the church is in error for having taught and for still teaching that in accordance with the evangelical and apostolic doctrine (cf Mk10:1; 1Cor 7), the marriage bond cannot be dissolved because of adultery on the part of one of the spouses, and that neither of the two, not even the innocent one who has given no cause for infidelity, can contract another marriage during the lifetime of the other; and that the husband who dismisses an adulterous wife and marries again and the wife who dismisses an adulterous husband and marries again are both guilty of adultery, anathema sit.' Quoted from *The Christian Faith in the Doctrinal Documents of the Catholic Church*, edited by J Neuner and J Dupuis (London: Collins Liturgical Publications, 1983), 529.

God's Dreaming:
Tomorrow's Roman Catholic Church

Antony F Campbell, SJ

Change has affected today's global world as seldom before. Global media have made this obvious to all who can see. The people, men and women, who are the Church are affected by this change. It would be impossible for change not to affect the Church. Much has occurred; more is on the way. King Canute could not hold back the sea; Rome cannot hold back the change.

To my mind, there are five BASIC areas where immediate change is needed in the Roman Catholic Church today. There are many others, but these five are basic.

1. The abolition of cardinals, their status and prerogatives.
2. The equality of women: being a woman as no obstacle for any position in the Church.
3. The revision of the status of pope: leader not monarch.
4. The recognition of the people of God as the core of the Church.
5. The recognition of God's love for us humans, sinners as we are, as the cause of the Incarnation.

Reducing these to something like a short summary might seem harsh and divisive. What the summary does is give a hint of the outcome of the comments below. Here are the soundbites:

No need for cardinals
Great need for women
Revision needed for papacy
Revaluation needed for people of God
'Loved though sinners' to replace 'guilt & sin'

Unpacking these briefly:

Cardinals have to go because they are too easily perceived as constituting a papal court, subtly emphasising the view of the pope as monarch. Monarchy and clericalism are the major flaws on today's Roman Catholic Church. Beyond the roles of bishop and archbishop, there would need to be some form of recognition for specific service to the Church. For example, Counsellor to the Pope (CP) and Advisor to the Pope (AP), and others.

The statement that being a woman or being female is no obstacle for any position within the Church is not to ignore that there are other obstacles beyond gender to specific positions within the Church. Such obstacles could be lack of experience, lack of knowledge, lack of the personal qualities required, lack of training and preparation, and so on. But being woman or being female is not an obstacle.

Currently the pope, once elected, is in power for life and that power is nominally absolute. The latter two qualities, life term and absolute power, are shared only with dictators, tyrants, and despots—not good company for a pope. That the pope is elected is essential, but not for life, and not by a College of Cardinals that has never been meant to be representative of the global Church.

With the cardinals gone, a new electoral college is required to elect the Pope. Such an electoral college should reflect the people of God, men and women, with one or more members from each bishops' conference, including the people, men and women, within the region of each conference. The college would elect the pope for a fixed term (say five or ten years). At the end of such a term, an electoral college would be reassembled with a simple mandate: whether to retain or replace the current pope. If replacement is decided, a new pope would need to be elected. In this way, the pope is the servant and leader of the people of God, not their monarch.

Doctrinal issues and the like within the Church, are not to be determined by the decision of the pope or the curial bureaucracy. Akin to the electoral college there would need to be an ecclesial college, representing the entire people of God, men and women, and convening as needed to advise their leader, the pope, on matters concerning the people of God. Decisions needed after the work of an ecclesial college would be the task of the pope as leader of the people of God.

Guilt has long been in the background of so much language of God correlated with divine mercy. With scriptural evidence for the notion of original sin largely dismissed, attention needs to shift to the issue of God's love for the sinner, all sinners. A focus on sin and guilt and redemption detracts from the mystery of the Incarnation and is unfair to God and untrue to God. It is the triumph of the human obliterating the mystery of the divine.

What I have briefly outlined needs to be unfolded in more detail. One way of thinking about the Church is that it is a precious vessel into which we pour our need for meaning, our longing for the spiritual, and our response to a loving God. The Church is a vessel, a sphere of life, in which those values are revered and are energised, in which lives are lived that embody those values. The Church is not merely something that happened to us: I was born Catholic; I went to a Catholic school; I was Catholic/I am Catholic. More than that: the Church is something that I chose as I matured and as these values became important to me. The Church is the sphere of life where I find the values that I hold dear sustained and cherished—and so energized and kept alive in me. There I find others who cherish the same values and whose friendship energises these values and keeps them alive in me.

The Church is today's response to the reality of Jesus Christ. We moderns need to be aware of the full impact of this reality, of the wonder and awe it involves. In the early years of the Church's existence theologians struggled with the task of finding language to express adequately the fact of Jesus Christ. There was but one God, yet Jesus was the Son of God, and Jesus spoke of the Holy Spirit. Trinitarian theology was developed to cope with this. Beyond the idea of a Trinity, the life of Jesus as one of us was evidence of the value God set then and sets now on human life—God's concern for us, and God's commitment to us, and our wonder and awe in response. It was also evidence of how a human life could be lived.

Centuries went by as the Church struggled for suitable language to express these beliefs. The outcome was the great early Councils such as Nicaea, Ephesus, Chalcedon, and Constantinople. Their work is not surpassed today. The Nicene Creed (or equivalent) is an integral part of the weekly Roman Catholic liturgy. Over the centuries, however, it has never taken away the absolute mystery of Christian faith. Over the years, the vessel has needed refining and restructuring; after all, there have been aberrations. Today the vessel acutely needs reshaping in order to be faithful to its past.

The vessel also needs reshaping in order to achieve its goals now. If the Church is to have a role as a significant body in people's lives, it has to energize what people value in their faith. The need for meaning can lead to contact with others and it can lead to seeking the ultimate contact with one's inner being. The longing for the spiritual can be met with others and with oneself in the context of a loving God and Jesus Christ, God's Son. The recognition of God's love for us is most present in the person of Jesus Christ. Contact with tomorrow's Church is at its best deeply and richly human. Support is there when support is needed. Life is energized when energy is lacking. When human presence is needed, human presence is there. When human goodness is to be sought out and sustained, the contents of the vessel can be drawn on and give life. Does the sophistication of much of modern life sometimes distract us from the innerness of these realities?

In the right circumstances, three simple words, 'I love you', can have a transforming and totally joyful effect on a human being; wonder and awe approach it, but fall short. Hearing those words from God is far from simple, but it is the essence of modern Christianity. Ancient Israel enshrined it in Psalm 8:

> What are human beings that you are mindful of them,
> mortals that you care for them? (Ps 8:4)

'Wow!' falls far short of a human response. Yet it was said then and remembered; it still needs to be heard now and taken to heart. It is far from face to face expression, yet it is at the core of faith's reality. Many of us back off, but in our heart of hearts we know we shouldn't. Tomorrow's Church must place at its core that universal love, love for all—not by us for God, but of God for all people, all of us. As parents love their wayward kids, so does God love God's often wayward creation. The French saying is to the point: '*tout savoir est tout pardoner*' (to know all is to forgive all). God has the advantage of knowing all. Of course it is a mystery, but mysteries are to be treasured.

This essay seeks to address that reshaping. Five points are enough; others will flow from these.

Cardinals

Cardinals as princes of the Church go a long way back in history. The concept is not divorced from the feudalism of the late Middle Ages. The prince archbishop is not an unusual figure from those times. Reading John O'Malley's *Trent*,[1] I was surprised to realise that alongside so important and so extensive a Council attention had to be paid, beyond the bishops, to four monarchs: the Holy Roman Emperor, the King of France, the King of Spain, and of course the pope (King of the Church). The interaction of Church and State power goes back centuries. Over the centuries, the role of the pope as monarch is evident. Over the centuries, the role of cardinals has evolved. Today, whatever their status in canon law, they can be seen as a princely court surrounding the pope, with privileged access to the pope, and with higher standing than many in the governing circles of the Church.

If the model of leadership in the RC Church is to be, as it should be, the washing of the feet (Jn 13; 'For I have set you an example' Jn 13:15), cardinals in their splendour have to go. It will be a loss for TV and the media, but it is loss that must be borne. The evolution of the papacy into a monarchy is undoubtedly a troubled and complex one requiring the attention of a professional historian—which I am not. That the evolution has arrived at a monarchy is beyond doubt.

The practical issues would need to be worked out. It is relatively simple for a pope to announce that he would no longer nominate any new cardinals. That leaves the situation uncertain for those already in place. One possibility might be to offer current cardinals the choice between their current job and the status of cardinal. Keep the status of cardinal and resign from the current job. Or keep the current job and resign from the position of cardinal. There would be other possibilities.

The leadership model I am using is that of a prime minister in the Westminster system. The prime minister is elected by his party. If he strays too far from his party, he will be replaced. The party is elected by the people. If it strays too far from the people, it will be

---

1. John W O'Malley, *Trent: What Happened at the Council* (Cambridge: Harvard University Press, 2013).

replaced. For the ways in which this might be achieved within the Roman Catholic Church, see below.

Women

Women make up at least fifty per cent of the human population around the globe. As a general rule, women have greater insight into matters religious than most men. The enormous contribution of women in the Roman Catholic Church is blindingly obvious, whether in schools, hospitals, social care, parishes, and so many other ways.

The idea that women should be excluded from certain positions within the Church can only be advocated from a position of patriarchy that cannot be sustained. Naturally certain positions require specific qualities and experience without which candidates would be excluded. Being female, being a woman cannot fall into this category.

So for example, if there is a search for a vicar-general, for a bishop, for a pope, certain qualities and abilities are required. If a man meets these requirements he can be a candidate; if he does not, he cannot be a candidate. Similarly, if a woman meets these requirements she can be a candidate; if she does not, she cannot be a candidate. Being male is not one of these requirements. It is an absurd waste that the Roman Catholic Church should deprive itself of access to fifty per cent of the talent available to it.

An aside: Does this mean that the current seminary system needs a thoroughgoing overhaul. According to what I have heard from those administering the system and those graduated from it, such an overhaul is needed. Trent is a long time ago; today is today. Access to university departments of theology is available now in ways that it never was before. The absence of access to effective pastoral priests is an unacceptable deprivation. One of the issues that today's Church authorities need to address urgently is what is needed in the formation of future priests and how this need can best be met. Theological education can be provided by departments of theology. Will this be comprehensive? Probably not. Is seminary theology comprehensive? Certainly not. A rethink and reshape is urgent.

Popes

If popes are to be leaders and not monarchs, some accountability towards those they lead is clearly essential. Two characteristics have to be mitigated: absolute authority and a life term. At first sight, it seems outrageous to suggest that popes are accountable to the people of God, men and women. But leaders are accountable to their people in ways more direct than those of monarchs. Vatican II is held up as an example of the people of God coming to the fore in the Roman Catholic Church. The role of the pope as monarch tends to remain behind the scenes. Reading the later Cardinal Yves Congar's account of the council (*My Journal of the Council*[2]) the evidence for this is constant and horrifying. A request is brought to the pope for a further title to be given to Mary. With the assembled Council present in Rome, Pope Paul VI quashed the request without the Council even knowing about it. The relationship between pope and council is a complex one. The pope is unquestionably a monarch, not the lesser status of a leader.

There is absolute authority and a life term. If the pope were elected for a limited term (five, or ten years, or whatever), subject to extension by an electoral college, the life term issue would be resolved. If extension of a limited term reflected accountability to the electoral college, less directly reflecting accountability to the people of God, the absolute authority issue would be resolved.

The proposal put forward here, therefore, is that in the absence of the cardinals, there should be an electoral college made up of one or two electors from each episcopal conference or a person from that region, outside the episcopal conference. The present electoral college of cardinals is hardly representative of the global Church. An electoral college drawn from the global spread of episcopal conferences has the possibility of being more globally representative. It has the *possibility*; many might say the *vain hope*. Those with hope and optimism have to say the possibility. Centuries might pass before the possibility becomes real.

When the limited term expired, the pope would be under the obligation to convoke an electoral college. It would face a simple question: whether to *retain* or *replace* the pope. If the college decided

2.   Yves Congar, *My Journal of the Council* (Adelaide: ATF Press,).

to retain the pope, the issue of term limit would need decision. If the college decided to replace the pope, the pope would be under the obligation to resign and a successor would be elected. In this way, the two issues of absolute authority and life term are resolved. Lurking behind this proposal is the understanding of the people of God, men and women, as the core of the Church.

People

At first sight, it may seem to many that the idea of papal accountability to the people of God is out of the question. From the outset, Peter is the rock on which the Church is to be founded (Mt 16:18). Is that rock to lead or to reign? The foot washing of John 13 offers one example. 'For I have set you an example, that you also should do as I have done to you' (Jn 13:15). Leaders are attentive to their people.

'At first sight' is an invitation to further seeing. Looking reflectively into the past of theological tradition, we uncover the principle, '*Lex orandi lex credendi*' (the law of prayer is the law of belief). The praying is done by the people, men and women; the believing is articulated by the theologians. The recent pope Benedict XVI—himself a professional theologian, Professor Joseph Ratzinger, Tubingen— spoke out impressively on this issue.

> God's people constitute the 'magisterium that precedes', to which theology later has to add depth and which theology has to accept on an intellectual plane. May theologians always listen to this fount of faith and safeguard the humility and simplicity of little ones![3]

The message is clear, remembering the roots of Benedict XVI as a professional theologian: the fount of faith is God's people, men and women. 'May theologians always listen to this fount of faith.'

This is nothing new. In terms of tradition, it stretches from at least the Council of Vatican II to St Augustine (see Lumen Gentium #12 and 1 John 2:20, 27). Whatever utterances of reverence may come from various people from time to time, any awareness of history makes it clear beyond any doubt that God is not in some special

---

3. Quoted with source in Gill *Have Life Abundantly* (Adelaide: ATF Press), 66.

way embodied in the Roman Catholic pope. Morals and doctrine have both been gravely tarnished in the past by papal behaviours and papal assertions. As Pope Francis has said several times, reality triumph over ideas, or perhaps better that experience triumphs over speculation associated with faith. Jesus was the incarnate Word of God not because of God's longing to be one with the bureaucrats and officials of the Church, bishops and pope included. The Incarnation is evidence for the unitive love of God for the people God joined in Jesus.

The Roman Catholic pope is the leader of the Roman Catholic people of God. The pope is installed in office by the institution of the Roman Catholic Church. As leader, the pope is responsible to the people of God. When there is question of not renewing the papal term of office, the thoughts of the electoral college responsible for this should be on the well-being and faith of the people of God rather than favour or disfavour of the institution's central bureaucrats. While this is more easily put into words than established as fact in the political reality of human behaviour, the words must be there, 'the people of God are the Church' and political reality must be brought into line with that.

All of this is why, when Rome is seeking real answers to live questions (as in the series of Synods), it is the people of God who must be heard by the Pope and not the Pope who, in the first instance, instructs the people of God. The divorce and remarriage issue is a good case in point. Should it be decided by aged celibates, mainly in Rome, with extensive experience in theology and absolutely no experience in marriage, divorce, and remarriage. If the decision goes to the people of God, world wide, it is probable that it would be a very complex outcome. It would then be the role of the Pope, as leader of the people of God, to see how best that complex outcome should be put into practice across the global Church—whether region by region, or resolution by delay, or trust in personal conscience, or whatever possibilities may emerge. If the people of God are unhappy with the papal decisions, then at term's end a new Pope can be chosen.

Is it likely that this might be messy? Of course. Frankly, is there anything that is genuinely human that is not messy?

The Guilt Issue

It is hardly surprising that Christians are deeply concerned about evil and have long seen the death of Jesus as eliminating the burden of that evil. In today's world, the global reach of television and the more individualised reality of social media mean that we have an awareness of the widespread existence of evil that is probably unique to today.

It is difficult to look back to the very beginnings. Choices were not legislated; they happened and were perpetuated. The initial choice of Peter as leader was unbelievably symbolic. As the rock on whom the Church was to be founded, his frailty and fallibility can hardly be bettered. 'Get behind me, Satan' and 'I tell you, I know not the man' is evidence enough that humanity will never be excluded. That means also that what was acceptable at the beginning may no longer be acceptable in tomorrow's world. That also means that what is in the New Testament reflects its time and that time is no longer today. For answers, we must look to today's questions. Today's answers are not found in the solutions of yesteryear. Oddly enough, fidelity requires flexibility. What was valued then may need to make room for what is valued now. Divinity did not replace humanity. Divinity, in Jesus Christ, became human.

Conclusion

There is obviously much more to be said about specific areas where change is necessary. The clerical involvement in the issues of child sexual abuse is obviously one of them. But the five changes proposed here are fundamental; from them much else can flow. The elimination of the cardinals and the limits on the papacy play down the monarchical aspect of the Roman Catholic Church today. The opening to women of every position in the Church is simply doing away with an obvious hangover from a patriarchal past that greatly impoverishes the Church. The emphasis on the core role in the Church of the people of God should do much to diminish the crippling effect of clericalism in today's Church, both on the part of clergy and on the part of the people of God. The theological insistence must be on God's love for the sinner to replace issues of redemption from sin. It may be God's dream. Whether it will be the reality of tomorrow's Roman Catholic Church we have yet to see.

Being Church Today
(Here Comes Everybody!)

William Morris

Centuries ago when map makers ran out of the known world before they ran out of parchment, they would sketch a dragon at the end of the scroll. This was a warning to the explorer that he/she would be entering unknown territory and at their own risk. Unfortunately, some explorers took this symbol literally and were afraid to push on to new worlds. Other more adventurous explorers saw the dragons as a sign of opportunity, a door to virgin territory.

Each of us has a mental map of the world in our heads that contains the information we use to guide ourselves in our day-to-day encounters. Like the maps of long ago, our mental maps also have dragons on them. These represent things that, for whatever reason, we don't want to do or push beyond. It is the fear of something that stops us. Sometimes these dragons are valid; sometimes, however, they prevent us from discovering something new. [1]

Fear comes from a need to be in control and is one of the most debilitating emotions there is; elections are won on fear, people are controlled by fear. Frank O'Loughlin in his book, *This Time of the Church*, speaks of the formula used throughout much of the history of the Church, 'Outside the Church, no salvation' as being 'very significant as a strong motivating force in keeping people faithful to the Church and it was a strong motive for mission activity'.[2] When we fear something or someone we stop living and all our relationships starting with ourselves become stunted.

We need to break out of the ghetto of suffocation that fear puts us in and breathe the air of the Spirit. We need to walk in the hope of Pope John XXIII who was shocked to discover what was being said by some people who saw nothing but ruin and calamity in the existing state of society. He said 'they are in the habit of saying that our age is much worse than past centuries; they behave as though history, which teaches us about life, had nothing to teach them, and as though, at the times of the past Councils, everything was perfect in the matter of Christian Doctrine, public behaviour and the proper freedom of the Church'. John XXIII expressed 'complete disagreement with the prophets of doom, who give news, only of catastrophes, as though the World was nearing its end . . . It is better to recognise the mysterious designs of divine Providence . . .'[3]

What the World needed and was waiting for, he said, was 'a leap forward towards a doctrinal penetration and a formation of consciences corresponding more completely and faithfully with the authentic doctrine . . .' Of that authentic doctrine he said: 'It is one thing to have the substance of the ancient doctrine of the Deposit of Faith but quite another to formulate and re-clothe it'.

> As we open this Council we see, as always, that the truth of Jesus is permanent. Often, as one age succeeds another, the opinions of people follow one another and exclude each other. Errors creep in, but vanish like fog before the sun. In the past we have opposed these errors and often condemn them. But today we prefer to make use of the medicine of Mercy rather than that of severity.'[4]

Pope John XXIII threw open the windows and doors with the expectation that the Spirit will come from any direction. Pope Francis has shown the same openness to the Spirit in his ministry to the world by using the medicine of Mercy and compassion: 'by moving towards others with a disarming humility and willingness to be vulnerable to criticism and even manipulation'. And 'prepared to open doors and build bridges without having a clear assurance of what might lie behind or beyond them',[5] being prepared to be surprised by the God of Surprises. He continually calls for dialogue and an openness of heart that leads to mercy that brings our hearts closer to the journey of others. Pope Francis wants to break the monologue of an Imperial Church by creating a dialogical Church defining itself as the 'The People of God' that 'is commissioned to announce the mercy of God, the beating heart of the Gospel.'[6] 'The Church's first truth is the love of Christ . . . (and) her language and her gestures must transmit mercy, so as to touch the hearts of all people and inspire them once more to find the road that leads to the Father.' [7]

The error would be to listen to the 'prophets of doom who are always forecasting disaster as though the end of the world was at hand' and lock the windows and doors in order to keep the Spirit within our house. That very action of locking doors and windows is fatal. For the Church is 'missionary by its very nature'[8] as taught by the Council and 'the spirit of Vatican II (demanded) that the Church should form and mould Christians in (the) spirit of the Gospels rather than make them perpetually dependent on externally imposed restrictions.'[9]

By the time the Bishops returned for the Second Session of Vatican II, John XXIII had died and Cardinal Montini had become Paul VI. At the opening Mass he stressed what had become apparent to most when he described the objectives of the council as 'the self-awareness of the Church; its renewal; the bringing together of all Christians in unity; the dialogue of the Church with the contemporary world'. Pope Francis has shown by his words and actions that this must be done openly, in the embrace of trust with a compassionate and merciful heart.

The Council participants reflected and they learnt as it went on. They never thought of it as the Council to end all Councils. At no time did it pretend to be saying the last word, and at the end of the last working of the Assembly there was no euphoria among the Council Fathers for there was acknowledgment that the work of renewal will never end this side of the grave. This renewal will only happen in openness to the Spirit, a trusting in the power that comes through the living Christ and a Christ-like love for all humanity. Archbishop Frank Rush spoke of a conversation he had with a Bishop from another country who had been saying the Council should change nothing. Rush suggested that maybe there was a need to remove obstacles and change attitudes that were 'hiding the face of Christ'.

Pope Francis in his Apostolic Exhortation, *Evangelii Gaudium* begins with 'The joy of the Gospel fills the hearts and lives of all who encounter Jesus'. It speaks of the Church as God's leaven in the midst of humanity, helping its aspirations and goodness to rise to the fore, relying always on the mercy and compassion of God.

Francis goes on to say:

> I prefer a Church which is bruised, hurting and dirty because
> it has been out on the streets, rather than a Church which is
> unhealthy from being confined and from clinging to its own
> security. More than by fear of going astray, my hope is that
> we will be moved by the fear of remaining shut up within
> structures which give us a false sense of security, within rules
> which make us harsh judges, within habits that make us feel
> safe, while at our door people are starving and Jesus does not
> tire of saying to us: 'Give them something to eat' (Mk 6:37).[10]

In an article in *The Tablet* of 6 September 2014, 'Preparing for the Synod
on the Family', John O'Malley pointed out that Pope Francis was the
first pope in first years not to have participated in the Second Vatican
Council. O'Malley believed that this was an advantage, for, unlike his
immediate predecessors, he (was) a non-combatant, above the fray
that is still vivid in the minds and hearts of the Councils participants.
(For) in comparison with them, he sites Council documents less
frequently—because, it seems, he has so well understood and so
serenely appropriated the Council's basic orientations that they are
completely natural to him.

This is what Karl Rahner SJ was hoping for, that it would be the
task of each generation to proceed from where the Council left off.
For he insisted that Vatican II was not a point of arrival, but 'a point
of departure', and 'the mission (of the Church) was to complete its
unwritten agenda by means of a theopraxis that (was) commensurate
with its new orientation.[11] New language needed to be found for only
in time would the Documents come alive when language developed,
and lived experience would keep giving them new life in the life and
light of the culture of the day.

It was the paradigm of renewal rather than reform that was the
framework for the implementation of Vatican II. The challenge was
to transpose the Council's vision into continuous renewal according
to the needs of the times and places, but always according to the
Council's own vision of Church expressed as the People of God. This
was a structural change from a hierarchical model, to a Communion
of God's People. This was a paradigm shift.

This model involved the universal call to holiness (*Lumen Gentium*
39–42). 'Which means that there are no holier classes in the Church

but that there is a variety of ways in which each category of persons attains holiness according to the calling (they) received from God'. It involves the Common priesthood of the faithful (*Lumen Gentium* 10–11):

> which points to the entire Church or God's People as a 'priestly community' in which the ministerial priesthood is given an 'essentially' different role not necessarily a superior role, so that both categories participate in the 'one priesthood of Christ', each in its own way. The ritual role of the ministers is contrasted with the priestly exercise of the laity in their daily life.

Aloysius Pieris SJ calls it the 'Liturgy of Life' to capture the common baptismal priesthood as described in Lumen Gentium. Cyprian of Carthage, third century Saint says, *Christianus alter Christus* (Every Christian is another Christ). It also involves a Common indefectible faith of God's People or *sensus fidelium* (common sense of the faithful) which is described in (*Lumen Gentium* 12) as the exercise of the 'prophetic role of Christ' according to the anointing by the Holy Spirit so that the 'universal body of the faithful' (bishops, priests and laity all together) 'cannot be mistaken in belief'. The 'guidance by the sacred magisterium' as well as 'obedience to it' is contextualized within this common participation of all God's People in the prophetic role of Christ, that is, in the common indefectibility of the Faithful. [12]

Collegiality, of all the issues in dispute in Council discussions, this one was most fiercely opposed by the minority, for they realised that more than any other single provision of the Council, it defined how the Church was to operate in the future—not as a monarchy, with all authority flowing from above, but as a collegial body that accomplishes its mission under a servant leader.[13] The Church was to act in a way that would reflect its reality as the People of God. The model was a circle not a pyramid and leadership was to be Lateral not Vertical, making 'the church (as Pope Francis has asked for) into an inverted pyramid in which the hierarchy is not on top but underneath, supporting the laity'.[14] This vision of collegiality—the papal governing of the Church in collaboration with the bishops of the world—still has not been achieved.

Francis writes in *Evangelii Gaudium*: 'Being Church means being God's people, being God's leaven in the midst of humanity—as I have already pointed out—the Church must be a place of mercy freely given, where everyone can feel welcomed, loved, forgiven and encouraged to live the good life of the Gospel.'[15] And then he says pointedly to each of us: 'I ask you to adopt in every activity, which you undertake, a missionary heart, (which) never closes itself off, never retreats into its own security, never opts for rigidity and defensiveness. It always does what good it can, even if in the process, its shoes get soiled by the mud of the street.'[16]

Being church then means '(being) the beating heart of the Gospel',[17] to model new relationships, a vision that has long played itself out in the hearts of many as they lose themselves in the relationship of love with God and become God's partners in the work of love, co-creators.

It is in the living of life, it is in relationships, that the gifts of the Spirit are enfleshed; in compassion, mercy, forgiveness, justice, peace, truth, love, hope; we grow not through exercising power over one another but by kindness, attachment, inclusiveness, collaboration and according to Francis—encounter—by listening to one another and making space for one another.[18] God emerges out of relationships of love, which is the divine, creative intrinsic principle and the source of God in Creation,[19] celebrated in the Dialogue of Salvation. This dialogue is spoken of by Pope Paul VI in his Encyclical Letter, *Ecclesiam Suam* (The Church in the Modern World).

For Paul VI it is 'a dialogue which God the Father initiated and established with us through Christ in the Holy Spirit . . . (which) we must examine closely if we want to understand the relationship which we, the Church, should establish and foster with the human race.'[20] Paul VI goes on to point out that, 'God himself takes the initiative in the dialogue of salvation. 'He hath first loved us' (1 Jn 4:10). We, therefore, must be the first to ask for a dialogue with men (and women), without waiting to be summoned to it by others.'[21] The encyclical goes on to point out that this dialogue does 'not depend on the merits of those with whom it (is) initiated, nor on the results it would be likely to achieve' setting no 'limits to our dialogue or seek in it our own advantage'.[22] For this dialogue springs 'from the goodness and love of God'.[23] and God emerges out of relationships of love.[24] This leads to 'no physical pressure (to be used) on anyone to accept the dialogue of salvation . . . it's an appeal of love . . . (and all are) left free to respond to it or reject it.'[25] It is accessible to all without distinction, universal (cf Col 3:11). [26]

Karl Rahner SJ explains: 'God does not merely create something other than himself—He also gives himself to this other. The World receives God, the Infinite and ineffable mystery, to such an extent that he himself becomes its innermost life.'[27] We have to find ways to make this mystery visible so it vibrates with the hearts and minds of our sisters and brothers today. We have to remove obstacles and change attitudes that 'hide the face of Christ'.

I believe this age needs to be the Age of the Word, not Dogma or Law. I am not saying these aren't important, but the gifts of the Spirit are essential for the Word to permeate the cultures of every age, giving us a lens through which to view creation and tradition with vision, leaving the future open to change, open to the creative freedom of each generation but always in the vision of the Church as the People of God, the mode given to us by the Vatican Council.

Many historians have attributed the change in language between Vatican II and Vatican I to the writings of Cardinal John Henry Newman and the Council's outgoing, optimistic and inclusive approach to his influence. Robert McClory pointed out that in Newman's view the Church's teaching could not be a top down one-way street. It must be a 'breathing together' of the faithful and their pastors, a cooperative venture. The teaching Church, before teaching, must discover what the believing Church really believes, so that the believing Church 'recognises' as authentic that which is presented to it as doctrine. When the believing Church does not recognise teaching it is clear that the necessary breathing together has not occurred.

Newman stressed that this in no way undercuts the authority of the teaching Church which has responsibility for wading prayerfully and cautiously through this tangle of sources. But he added of all the sources 'I am accustomed to lay stress on *consensus fidelium*'. [28] You (we) are that voice, you (we) are the Church.

Now what is 'characteristic of all renewal is that it starts as an event necessitated by circumstances in the margin of an institution (society) before it vindicates its legitimacy as a reform accepted by the centre.'[29] In viewing Vatican II as a renewalist Council, 'it is the nature of a renewalist Council to leave the future open to change which is to say, open to the creative freedom of each generation'[30] as we listen with the Ears of *Scripture,(the Word), Tradition with Vision* (Tradition without vision leads us away from the Truth) *and Creation* (the World around us), in openness to the Spirit.

To be able to see this we need as individuals and as community to go through some form of 'Exile' – where there is a break because that is where the light gets in and growth happens.

Henri Lacordaire OP reflects: 'I have long thought that the most favourable moments for sowing and planting are times of trouble and storm.'

In exile we have to redefine who we are and it could be said that as a Church we are in exile today from both within and without. From within, because the believing Church and the teaching Church are not breathing together or are having trouble breathing together, and from without because we live in a culture which is both pluralistic and secular and in *Evangelii Nuntiandi*, Pope Paul VI suggests that the split between the Gospel and culture is the drama of our time just as it was of other times.

In our culture today we cannot take it for granted that people believe in the existence of God as they did in the time of the Prophets, as they did in the world Jesus lived in. Albert Nolan in his book *Jesus Today*, points out that our culture has 'generated a great gulf between ourselves and the people of the first century Palestine. One of those principal differences is that Jesus and his Jewish contemporaries took it for granted that God was a person. Today we can no longer take that for granted. Many people have difficulty with the idea of a personal God.' [31]

When the people of Israel were taken into Exile in Babylon between the years 587–538 BC, the prophets' role was to open up a highway, to give them hope, to free them from the absolute present, to give them a reference point outside their present culture. To give them hope that they were loved and not abandoned, to help them remember the past, that they are God's children, God is their Father, and in the middle of all that was happening to them they would be going back. Life would be different, for life in exile had changed them, their encounter with the Babylonian culture had changed them, giving them a different vision of the Law (the Torah) that was more inclusive and filled with a wisdom they did not have before their Exile.

'The wise . . . are always formed in the testing ground of exile when the customary and familiar are taken away and they must go much deeper and much higher for wisdom.' [32] The Prophet Isaiah wrote in exile: Bring forward the people that is blind, it has eyes, that is deaf and yet has ears . . . No need to recall the past, No need to think about what was done before. See, I am doing something new! Even now before it comes to light, can you not see it? (43:8, 18–19)

The Second Vatican Council gave the world, gave the Church, a different vision of what being Church means, what being Catholic means in the full sense of the word. Ilia Delio in her book, 'The Emergent Christ', reminds us that 'to be Catholic is to be a "whole maker", to unite what is separate, and thus to evolve towards greater unity.' [33] It means dialogue with the contemporary world, the bringing together of all Christians in unity, a renewal, challenging us to transpose the Council's vision into continuous renewal according to the needs of the times and the places, but always according to the Council's vision of Church, relating it to all humankind. This was all done in the hope that as obstacles were removed and attitudes changed, that 'the face of Christ' may become more visible and the cry of mercy not sacrifice may be heard more clearly. 'Go and learn what this means, "I desire mercy, not sacrifice." For I have come to call not the righteous but sinners' (Mt 9:13).

So being Catholic (to be a 'whole maker') today means pointing to a vision beyond the present conventional wisdom of the day to an alternative wisdom based on justice, mercy, compassion, love, and hope which are constitutive to the gospel, '(weaving) a seamless garment', [34] and pointing to the dignity and equality of all peoples, leading us to recognise that our humanity precedes our religious identity, whatever that identity may be and our 'Interdependence obliges us to think of one World with a common plan'. [35]

Frank O'Louglin speaks of an understanding of Church that is set out in the documents of the Second Vatican Council, 'as relating the Church to the rest of humankind; it is set deliberately within humanity almost as an organ of humanity. They are set in intrinsic relationship with each other. The Church exists for the sake of humankind. In fact one can only understand the Church adequately by seeing it in its relationship to humankind.' [36] Stephen Bevans and Roger Schroeder following the lead of *Redemptoris Missio* 44 points to the truth 'that the explicit, prophetic proclamation of the Gospel and about Jesus has a certain "paramount priority", it is equally true that the words of proclamation must be rooted in an authentic being of Church . . . and in dialogue. The Church is called equally to incarnate what it says in its community life and in its engagement in the world.'[37]

Stephen Bevans SVD, in an article entitled: 'The Mission has a Church, the Mission has Ministers' reflects on the fact that the Church does not so much have a mission as the mission has a Church. The Church is not about itself. It is about the Reign of God that it preaches, serves and witnesses to . . . and if such is the case, any structure of leadership in the Church serves by helping it to be faithful to God's mission, for "mission precedes the Church".'[38]

'God's ever present Spirit took concrete form in Jesus of Nazareth and the Spirit's mission becomes his', revealing God's hidden action in the World. Now 'as the Spirit had anointed Jesus at the start of his ministry (Lk 4:16–21) so Jesus sent the Spirit upon his followers, (the community) who began to call themselves the Church . . . Jesus' very bodily presence in the world . . . created by and a dwelling place for the Spirit.' Bevans points out that this is in line with the thinking of Vatican II, who called the people of God, a Pilgrim Church, that is missionary by its very nature (*Ad Gentes* 2). The twentieth century German theologian Emil Brunner put it so beautifully in these words, 'the Church exists like mission as a fire exists by burning'. [39]

Bevans then goes on to say that as the Church's very nature is missionary:

> Mission comes first. The Church does not have a mission. The mission, rather, has a Church. The mission is first that of God's mission—through the Spirit, in Christ. We have been called into the Church to share and continue that mission. The Church exists not as an answer but as a response—a response to God's call to continue God's loving, redeeming, healing, reconciling, liberating, forgiving and challenging mission.[40]

As Bevans and Schroeder point out in their book *Prophetic Dialogue*, the Mission has a Church, that is the Mission has us,[41] and our gifts are intended for engagement. They carry within them an explicit invitation to become co-creators.

For this to happen Pope Francis asks that: 'Rather than experts with dire predictions, dour judges bent on rooting out every threat and deviation, we should appear as joyful messengers of challenging proposals, guardians of the goodness and beauty which shine forth in a life of fidelity to the Gospel.'[42] '(We) then make present the fragrance of Christ's closeness and his personal gaze.' [43]

Evangelisation, Pope Paul VI points out in *Evangelii Nuntiandi* (20), always begins with women and men and the relationship they have with their cultures. 'The Gospel, and therefore evangelisation, is certainly not identical with culture and they are independent in regard to all cultures. Nevertheless the Kingdom which the Gospel proclaims is lived by men (and women) who are profoundly linked to a culture, and the building up of the Kingdom cannot avoid borrowing the elements of human culture and cultures. Though independent of cultures, the Gospel and evangelisation are not necessarily incompatible with them; rather they are capable of permeating them all without becoming subject to any of them. The split between the Gospel and culture (the socialisation process of the past is no longer at work) is without a doubt the drama of our time, just as it was of other times. Therefore every effort must be made to ensure a full evangelisation of culture, or more correctly of cultures. They have to be regenerated by an encounter with the Gospel but this encounter will not take place if the Gospel is not proclaimed' and the best way of proclaiming the Gospel is living it.

'The living Gospel is to be found throughout history above all in the lives of flesh and blood Christians.' Edward Schillebeeckx OP goes on to say that, 'The account of the life of Christians in the world in which they live is a *fifth Gospel*; it also belongs at the heart of Christology.'[44]

The Church has to listen and re-listen to the Gospel and allow the Gospel to keep renewing it and reforming it from within. (c/f Evangelii Nuntiandi 15)

German Theologian Wolfhart Pannenberg made a poignant observation: 'Religions die when their lights fail', that is, 'when their teachings no longer illuminate life as it is actually lived by their adherence'. Elizabeth Johnson in *Quest for the Living God* makes this observation: 'In such cases, the way the Holy is encountered stalls out and does not keep pace with changing human experience . . . Some people will cling to the old views, but eventually most will move on, seeking ultimate meaning in a way that is coherent with their current experience of life. Then the lights of the old religion dim out; the deity becomes irrelevant.'

'This is not a case of human beings dictating to God what they want in a deity, as some fear.' Rather, Pannenberg argues, 'it is a test of the true God. Only the living God who spans all times can relate to historically new circumstances as the future continuously arrives. A tradition that cannot change cannot be preserved. Where people experience God as still having something to say, the lights stay on.' [45]

'I invite all Christians everywhere at this very moment, to a renewed personal encounter with Christ, or at least an openness to letting him encounter them,' writes Pope Francis, '(So) whenever we take a step towards Jesus, we come to realise that he is already there, waiting for us with open arms'. [46]

For Francis: 'Anyone who has truly experienced God's saving love does not need much time or lengthy training to go out and proclaim that love'.[47] For 'thanks solely to this encounter with God's love, which blossoms into an enriching friendship, we are liberated from our narrowness and self-absorption. We become fully human when we become more than human, when we let God bring us beyond ourselves in order to obtain the fullest truth of our being'.[48] Moreover 'God has found a way to be united to every human being in every age'.[49] God is the heart and the beyond of everything, Teilhard de Chardin reminds us. God is the withinness of the withoutness of matter in evolution.[50]

Francis urges 'each of us (to) find ways to communicate Jesus, wherever we are'.[51] 'We should not think that the Gospel message must always be communicated by fixed formulations learned by heart or by specific words which express an absolutely invariable content. This communication (Evangelisation) takes place in so many different ways that it would be impossible to describe or catalogue them all.'[52]

So it should not be surprising to any of us when Francis says the first step in evangelising 'which is always respectful and gentle, is personal dialogue'[53] and quotes Pope Benedict XVI: 'Effective Christian witness is not about bombarding people with religious messages, but about our willingness to be available to others by patiently and respectfully engaging their questions and their doubts as they advance in their search for the truth and the meaning of human existence.'[54]

Francis' experience in Argentina taught him how important it would be for the whole Church to be involved in the Synodal process, if renewal was to happen and the Church's 'Gospel Witness' to remove obstacles and change attitudes that were 'hiding the face of Christ'. He also remarked that celebrating the Mass and praying with lay people at the Marian Shrine during that time 'gave the (Bishops) a live sense of belonging to our people, of the Church that goes forward as the people of God, of us Bishops as its servants'. (*The Tablet* 25 October 2014)

So it is no surprise that he says to Bishops in *Evangelii Gaudium*: 'He (the bishop) will sometimes go before his people, pointing the way and keeping their hope vibrant. At other times, he will simply be in their midst with his unassuming and merciful presence. Other times, he will have to walk after them, helping those who lag behind and—above all—allowing the flock to strike out on new paths. (He will) listen to everyone and not simply to those who would tell him what he would like to hear.'[55] (There go the people, I must follow them for I am their leader, Alexandre Ledru-Rowlin)

He then says of himself: 'Since I am called to put into practice what I ask of others, I too must think about a conversion of the Papacy. Pope John Paul II asked for help in finding "a way of exercising the primacy which, while in no way renouncing what is essential to its mission, is nonetheless open to a new situation". We have made little progress in this regard.'[56] Francis concludes: 'I encourage everyone to apply the guidelines found in this document (*Evangelii Gaudium*) generously and courageously, without inhibitions or fear.'[57]

Francis is inviting the whole Church to dialogue with him, to participate with him in the 'Dialogue of Salvation'. A dialogue he began on the day of his election, continued with the invitation to the world to help him prepare for the Synod on the Family. In his final address at the end of the first session of the Synod on 18 October 2014 he asked all to be aware of the temptations faced in all encounters of relationship, temptations faced in dialogue as one encounters different views. Temptations of inflexibility, to treat the symptoms and not the causes and the roots, not to see the heavy and unbearable burdens people carry, to bow down to a worldly spirit instead of purifying it and bending it to the Spirit of God, to think that we are owners of the faith instead of guardians, to use meticulous and soothing language that says nothing.

We are invited to be surprised by the God of Surprises: 'We need to look at our cities with a contemplative gaze, a gaze of faith which sees God dwelling in their homes, in their streets and squares. He dwells among them fostering solidarity, fraternity and the desire for goodness, truth and justice. This presence must not be contrived but found, uncovered.'[58]

'What is called for', Francis writes, 'is an evangelisation capable of shedding light on these new ways of relating to God, to others and to the World around us. It must reach places where new narratives and paradigms are being formed, bringing the word of Jesus to the innermost soul of our cities,'[59] so that obstacles are dismantled, attitudes are changed and the face of Christ becomes visible. Pope John XXIII saw his first duty: to walk alongside other men and women. Loving them and bringing the Gospel in their midst. May that be our walk too, as we play our part in the Dialogue of Salvation and help all to see the hidden presence of God as 'the heart and beyond of everything', creating a longing which is expressed beautifully in the words of John O'Donohue:

> Blessed be the longing that brought you here and quickens your soul with wonder.
>
> May you have the courage to listen to the voice of desire that disturbs you when you have settled for something safe.
>
> May you have the wisdom to enter generously into your own unease. To discover the new direction your longing wants you to take.
>
> May the forms of your belonging – in love, creativity and friendship be equal to the grandeur and the call of your soul.
>
> May the one you long for long for you.
>
> May your dreams gradually reveal the destination of your desire.
>
> May a secret Providence guide your thoughts and nurture your feelings.
>
> May your mind inhabit your life with the sureness with which your body inhabits the World.
>
> May your heart never be haunted by ghost-structures of old damage.

May you come to accept your longing as divine urgency.
May you know the urgency with which God longs for you.[60]

NOTES:

1. Roger Von Oech, *A Kick in the Seat of the Pants,* (San Francisco: Harper Collins), 71 from 'More of the Bests of Bits and Pieces', compiled and edited by Rob Gilbert (New Jersey: The Economics Press, Inc, 1997).
2. Frank O'Loughlin, *This Time of the Church* (Mulgrave: Garratt Publishing, 2012), 80, 81.
3. Bill Huebsch, *The Council Vatican II in Plain English* (Thomas More Publishing 1997), 87, 88.
4. Huebsch, *The Council Vatican II in Plain English*, 90, 91
5. Robert Meckens, *Pope Francis and the disarming courage to be vulnerable,* Global Pulse, 9 February 2016.
6. Pope Francis, *Misericordiae Vultus,* 12
7. Pope Francis, *Misericordiae Vultus,* 12
8. *Ad Gentes, Vatican Council II, Decree on the Church's Missionary Activity.*2
9. Aloysius Pieris, SJ *Give Vatican II a Chance* (Sri Lanka: Tulana Research Centre, 2010), 20.
10. Pope Francis, *Evangelii Gaudium,* 49
11. Pieris, *Give Vatican II a Chance,* 20,
12. Pieris, *Give Vatican II a Chance,* 37–38
13. *The Tablet* 6 September 2014 article by John O'Malley.
14. Philip Pullella, Article 18 October 2015 '*Pope says Church Needs More Decentralisation, Changes to Papacy',* Reuters
15. Pope Francis, *Evangelii Gaudium, 114*
16. Pope Francis, *Evangelii Gaudium,* 45
17. Pope Francis, *Misericordiae Vultus 12*
18. Ilio Delio, *The Emergent Christ,* (Maryknoll, New York: Orbis, 2011), 6.
19. Delio, *The Emergent Christ,* 51
20. Pope Paul VI, *Ecclesiam Suam* (The Church in the Modern World) No. 71
21. Pope Paul VI, *Ecclesiam Suam,* 72
22. Pope Paul VI, *Ecclesiam Suam,* 74
23. Pope Paul VI, *Ecclesiam Suam,* 73
24. Delio, *The Emergent Christ,* 51.
25. Pope Paul VI *Ecclesiam Suam,* 75. (The Church in the Modern World) No. 75
26. Pope Paul VI *Ecclesiam Suam,* 76

27. Karl Rahner, 'The Specific Character of the Christian Concept of God', in *Theological investigations* 21 (New York: Crossroads, 1988), 21:185–95

28. Robert McClory, *Faithful Dissenters* (Maryknoll, New York: Orbis, 2000), 46, 47, 48.

29. Pierls, *Give Vatican II a Chance*, 33.

30. Pieris, *Give Vatican II a Chance*, 30

31. Albert Nolan, *Jesus Today* (Maryknoll, New York: Orbis, 2006), 48.

32. Richard Rohr, *What the Mystics Know* (New York: The Crossroad Publishing Company, 2015), 119

33. Ilio Delio, *The Emergent Christ*, 6.

34. Stephen B Bevans and Roger P Schroeder, *Prophetic Dialogue* (Maryknoll, New York: Orbis, 2011), 67.

35. Pope Francis *Laudato Si'*, 164

36. O'Loughlin, *This Time of the Church*, 82.

37. Bevans and Schroeder, *Prophetic Dialogue*, 71.

38. Bevans and Schroeder, *Prophetic Dialogue*, 15

39. Emil Brunner, *The Word in the World* (London: SCM Press, 1931), 11.

40. Stephen Bevans, 'The Mission has a Church, the Mission has Ministers' 2010

41. Bevans and Schroeder, *Prophetic Dialogue,* 15.

42. Pope Francis, *Evangelii Gaudium,* 168

43. Pope Francis, *Evangelii Gaudium* 169

44. Ormond Rush in *From North to South: Southern Scholars Engage with Edward Schillebeeckx*, edited by Helen F Bergin OP (Adelaide: ATF Press, 2013), 3.

45. Elizabeth Johnson, *Quests for the Living God* (London: Continuum, 2011), 23.

46. Pope Francis, *Evangelii Gaudium,* 3

47. Pope Francis, *Evangelii Gaudium,* 120

48. Pope Francis, *Evangelii Gaudium,* 8

49. Pope Francis, *Evangelii Gaudium,* 113

50. Teilhard de Chardin, *Phenomenon of Man,* translated by Bernard Wall (New York: Harper and Row, 1959), 53-56

51. Pope Francis, *Evangelii Gaudium, 121*

52. Pope Francis, *Evangelii Gaudium,* 129

53. Pope Francis, *Evangelii Gaudium,* 128

54. Pope Francis, 'Everyone is a Neighbour', 24 January 2014

55. Pope Francis, *Evangelii Gaudium,* 31

56. Pope Francis, *Evangelii Gaudium,* 32

57. Pope Francis, *Evangelii Gaudium,* 33

58. Pope Francis, *Evangelii Gaudium,* 71

59. Pope Francis, *Evangelii Gaudium,* 74

60. John O'Donohue, *Benedictus* (Ealing UK: Bantam Press, 2007), 53.

Contributor List

Massimo Faggioli is a Church historian, Professor of Theology and Religious Studies at Villanova University (Philadelphia). He had been on the faculty at the University of St Thomas (St Paul MN) between 2009 and 2016, where he was the founding director of the Institute for Catholicism and Citizenship (2014–2015). His recent books are *Sorting Out Catholicism. Brief History of the New Ecclesial Movements* (Liturgical Press, 2014), *Pope Francis. Tradition in Transition* (Paulist Press, 2015), *A Council for the Global Church. Receiving Vatican II in History* (Fortress Press, 2015), *The Legacy of Vatican II*, edited by Massimo Faggioli and Andrea Vicini SJ (Paulist Press, 2015), *The Rising Laity. Ecclesial Movements since Vatican II* (Paulist Press, 2016).

Geraldine Doogue AO, is an Australian journalist and radio and television host. Doogue was the host of Radio National's *Life Matters* program for eleven years. She received a United Nations Media Peace Prize and two Penguin Awards for her role in ABC TV's coverage of the Gulf War. She has been the host of *Compass* on ABC TV since 1998 and *Saturday Extra* on Radio National.

Robert Mickens, is editor-in-chief of *Global Pulse*. Since 1986, he has lived in Rome, where he studied theology at the Pontifical Gregorian University before working 11 years at Vatican Radio and then another decade as correspondent for *The Tablet* of London.

Geoffrey Robinson, was an auxiliary Bishop for the Archdiocese of Sydney from 1984 to 2002. His published works include: *Marriage, Divorce and Nullity - A Guide to the Annulment Process in the Catholic Church* (Collins Dove, 1984), *Travels in Sacred Places* (HarperCollins Religious, 1997), *Confronting Power and Sex in the Catholic Church: Reclaiming the Spirit of Jesus* (Garratt Publishing, 2007 (US edition

Liturgical Press, 2008), *Love's Urgent Longings, Wrestling with Belief in Today's Church* (Garratt Publishing, 2010), *For Christ's Sake End Sexual Abuse in the Catholic Church for Good* (Garratt Publishing, Melbourne, 2013), *The 2015 Synod The Crucial Questions: Divorce and Homosexuality* (ATF Press, 2015).

Antony Campbell, is a Jesuit Priest, who taught Old Testament at Jesuit Theological College, Melbourne, from1974 to 2009 and author of numerous books and articles, including: *The Changing Face of Form Criticism for the Twenty-First Century* (Eerdmans, 20003), *God and the Bible* (Paulist Press, 2008), and *Experiencing* Scripture (ATF Press, 2012).

Bill Morris, was Bishop of the Diocese of Toowoomba, Australia, from 1992 to 2011. He is author of *Benedict, Me and the Cardinals Three* (ATF Press, 2014).

CPSIA information can be obtained
at www.ICGtesting.com
Printed in the USA
FFOW04n0005050117
30973FF